THE BANJOIST'S BUDGET

[1883]

CONTAINING

FIFTY JIGS, REELS, HORNPIPES, CLOGS, WALK-AROUNDS, ETC

CORRECTLY ARRANGED AND FINGERED FOR THE BANJO

FOR PROFESSIONAL OR AMATEUR USE

BY

A. BAUR

EDITED AND INTABULATED

BY ROB MACKILLOP ©2011

CAN BE PLAYED IN STROKE STYLE, MELODIC CLAWHAMMER STYLE, OR FINGER STYLE

Online Audio

To access the online audio recording go to:
WWW.MELBAY.COM/30824MEB

WWW.MELBAY.COM

Contents

Contents

Albert Baur (184? – 1920)

Albert Baur's *The Banjoist's Budget* contains some of the most interesting 19th-century banjo music. There seem to be four main strands of repertoire therein: minstrel, Irish, clog dancing, and Gilbert & Sullivan arrangements. The music can be played using the old minstrel stroke technique, as detailed in Frank B. Converse's *Analytical Banjo Method* of 1887, or with the modern melodic clawhammer technique (with much use of the thumb on all strings), or fingerstyle, as exemplified again in Converse's *Analytical.*

Baur clearly started his banjo life as a minstrel-style player, and learned the art of the popular entertainer while in the Union army. From "Reminiscences of a Banjo Player", "Banjo and Guitar Journal", February, 1893,

> "...In 1864 there were very few regiments in the service that had more than one wagon for the whole regiment... Strict orders were at all times issued that no baggage must be carried for an enlisted man in any of the wagons... Where there's a will, there's a way, and a few of us managed with the help of a friendly teamster to stow away a tackhead banjo and an accordion...
>
> If the weather was pleasant a crowd would gather around the camp fire, the banjo and accordion having been sneaked out of the wagon and a door from some farm house or a couple of boards having been put on the ground on one side of the fire, the audience would take its place on the opposite side, when the evenings entertainment would be gone through with. It consisted of songs with banjo and accordion accompaniment, stories of home and jig dancing. The performances were crude but helped while away many a lonely hour and remind us of home and friends in the far north.
>
> Owing to poor facilities for keeping the instruments in order, the instrumental part of our entertainments were always the poorest. Sometimes it would be weeks before we could get a (banjo) string, and if the banjo head was broken, it took much time and manoeuvring for one of our party to steal into the tent of a drummer and punch a hole in a drum (head) near the shell, after which we would watch that drummers tent with eagle eyes until he took the damaged head and threw it out, when one of the gang would pounce on it and bring it to camp in a round about way. Owing to their thickness, the drum heads did not make very good banjo heads, but they beat nothing clear out of sight. In addition to the banjo and accordion, we had a set of beef bones and a sheet iron mess pan answered for a tambourine. Taking into consideration our surrounding and the disadvantages under which we labored, we had some tolerably good shows and at any rate satisfied our open air audiences..."

"Minstrel Stage Reel", and the various "walk around" dances have clear references to the minstrel tradition. In a walk around, the performers would leave the stage and walk into the audience, performing as they go. Baur's last tune must have been a popular 'final number' of an evening's entertainment: "Roll Down the Curtain Walk Around" – which was doubtless accompanied by much clapping and whooping from the audience.

Much has been written of black-face minstrelsy, and rightly so, but the comic lampooning of the Irish was, in many communities, just as popular. *The Banjoist's Budget* contains many Irish-related tunes. See my *Early Irish-American Banjo* (Mel Bay Publications) for more details.

Some of the oddest tunes in the book are the **clog dances**. The history of clog dancing is many-stranded, with roots in the immigrant populations of the Appalachians: Scots, Irish, Dutch, German, etc. Some point to the Blackfoot Indians as a possible source. We can say with some certainty that its popularity spread as a reaction against the more regimented forms of square dancing. In clog dancing, there is a high degree of self expression, and the odd rhythms and surprising melodic contours of the tunes collected by Baur, back this up. One should not assume that dancing with wooden shoes was always a noisy affair, but could be, as some of the titles here seem to suggest, "Light and Airy", "Neat and Graceful", and "Aesthetic".

It is hard to overestimate the popularity of the songs from Gilbert & Sullivan operettas during the 1880s, and it is little wonder that Baur's collection reflects this. View these tunes as arrangements of the pop songs of the day.

So, there is plenty of scope for themed programs for today's performer, and much for the social historian to get his or her teeth into. Baur gives no technique instructions, and the music sounds well whichever way you choose to play it, with either down or up picking. He is very precise in his notation of pull-offs, but there is curiously not one hammer-on in the entire publication. I have chosen to leave the decision to include them up to you.

Tuning: Baur's notation indicates eAEG♯B, which translates into a modern pitch of gCGBD. I have found though that many of the pieces are easier to play if the 4th string is tuned up a tone to either eBEG♯B or gDGBD. So, wherever I give the indication 'High 4th', it is editorial, and you have the choice of playing the TAB as written, or making the notes on the 4th string two frets higher.

Enjoy!

Rob MacKillop
Edinburgh, 2020

The Banjoist's Budget

Edited by
Rob MacKillop

A. Baur, 1883

1. Minstrel Stage Reel

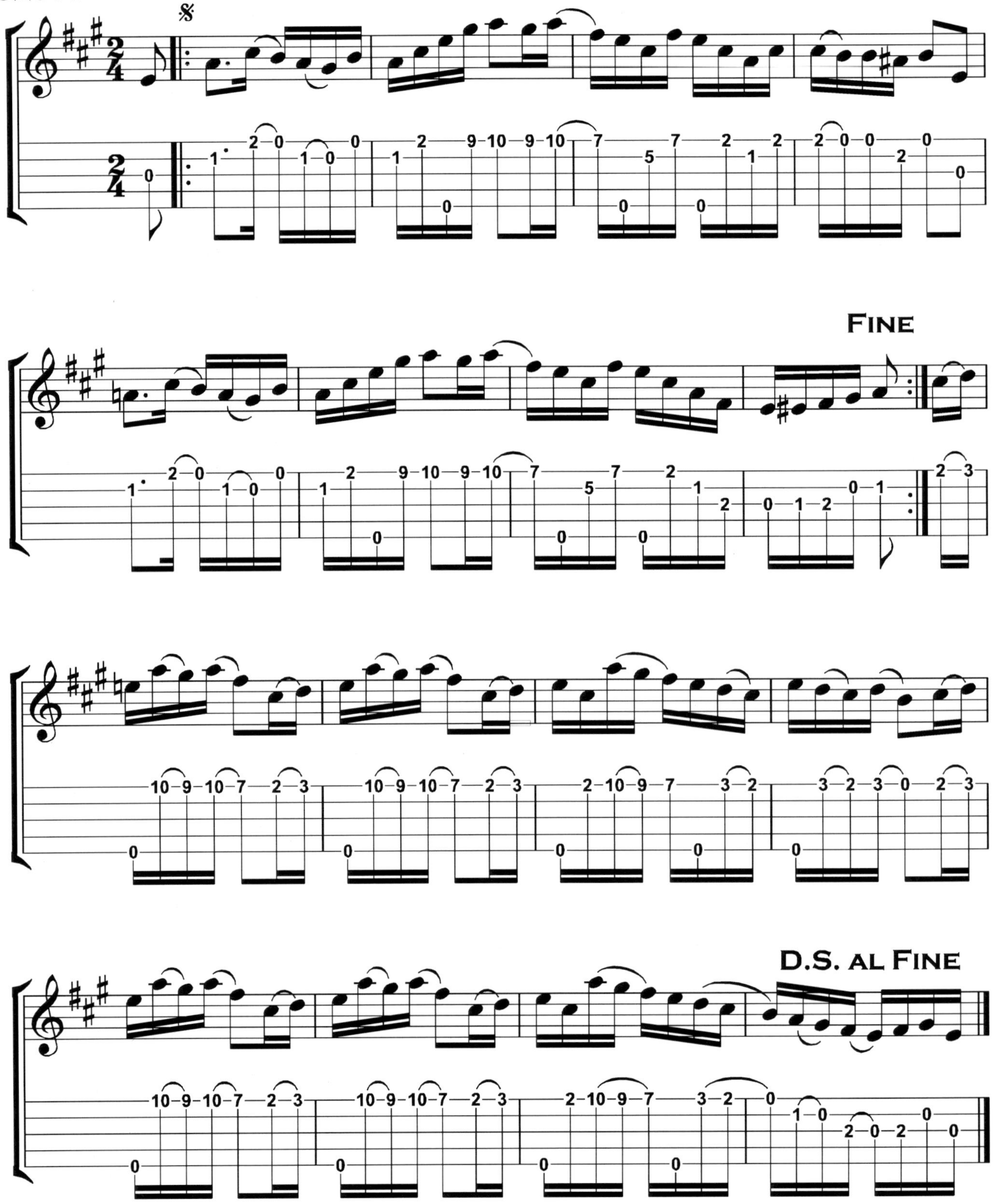

Fine

D.S. al Fine

2. Muldoon Irish Reel

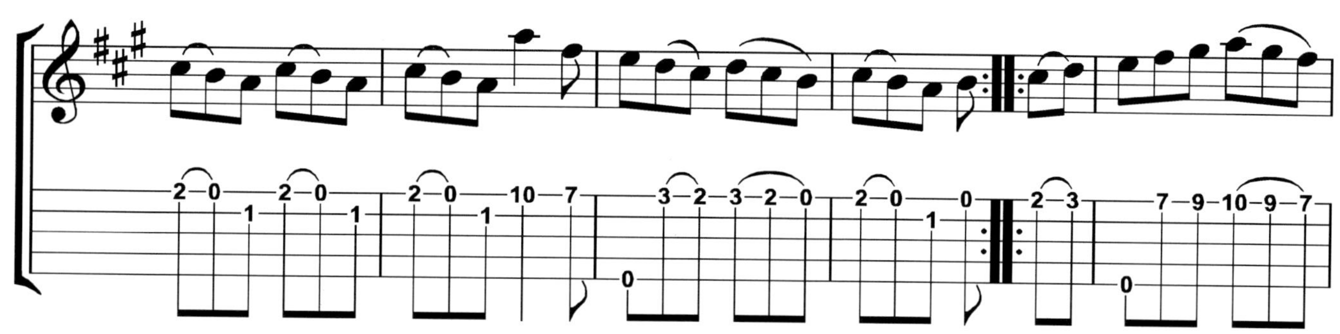

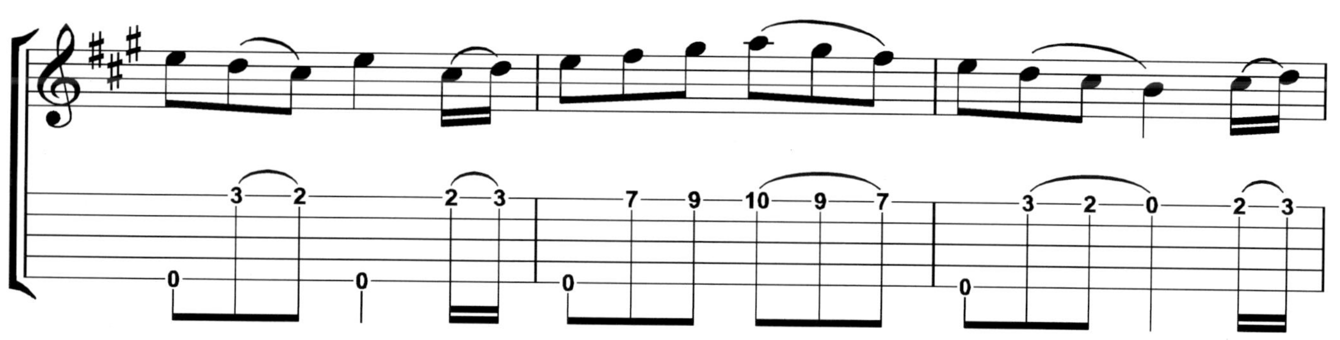

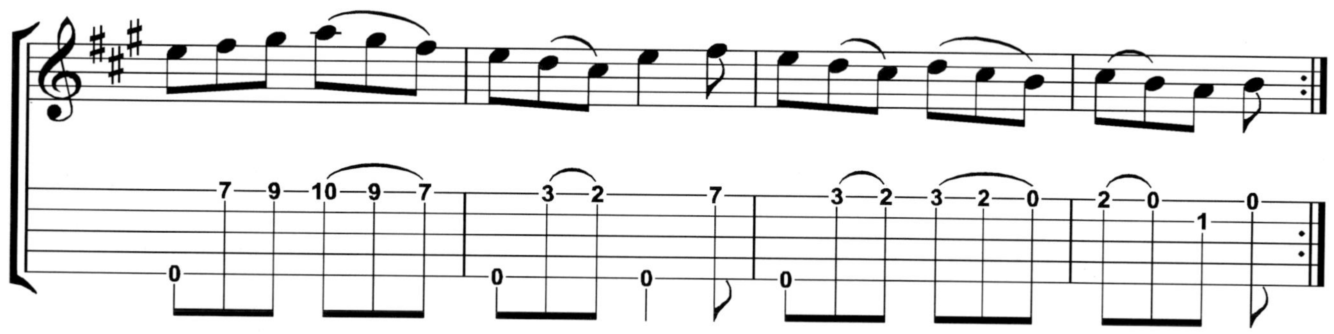

3

3. On Deck Hornpipe

4
4. The Captain Hornpipe
1.
2.

5. Nobody Knows Reel

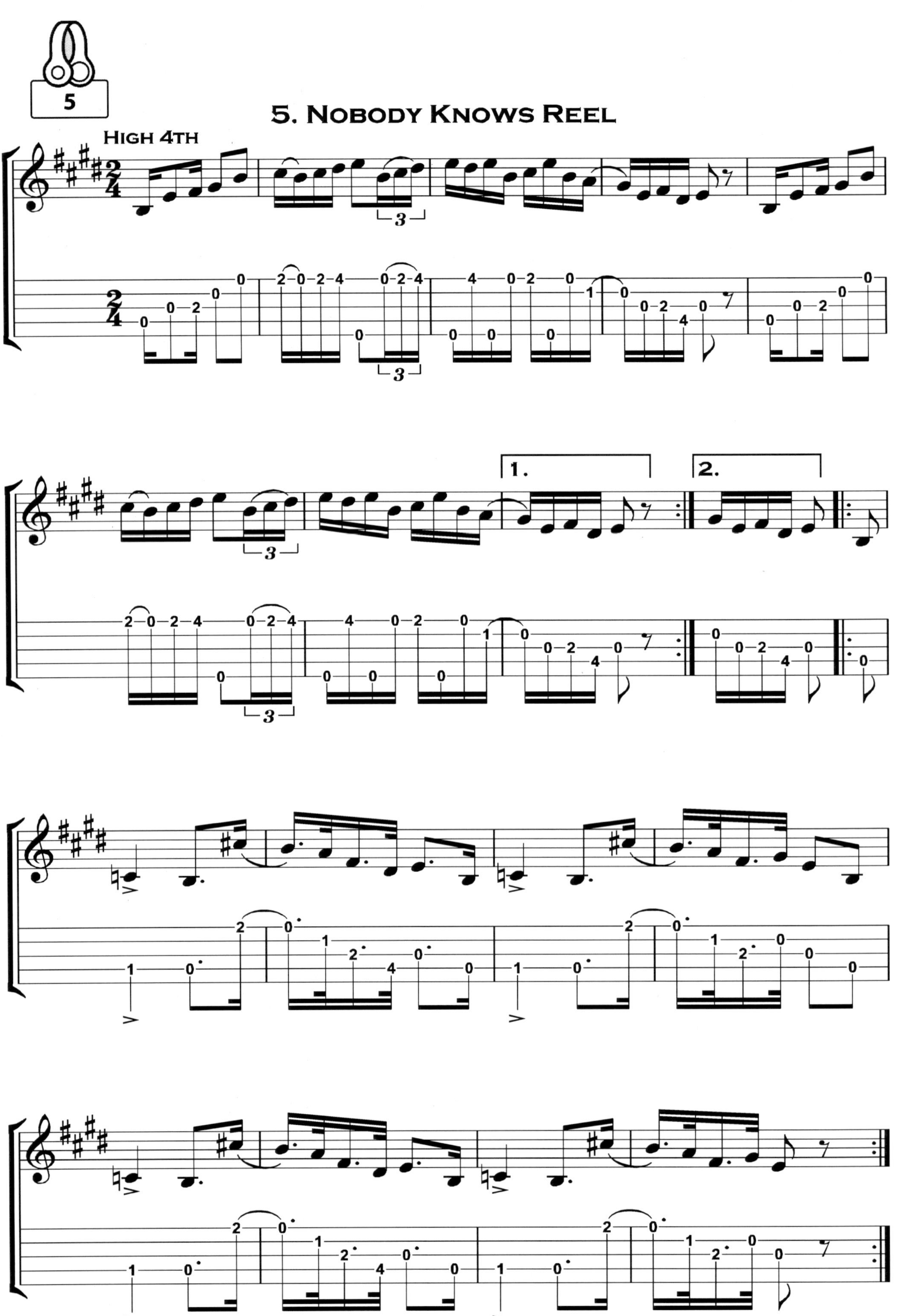

6. Dancers Delight Hornpipe

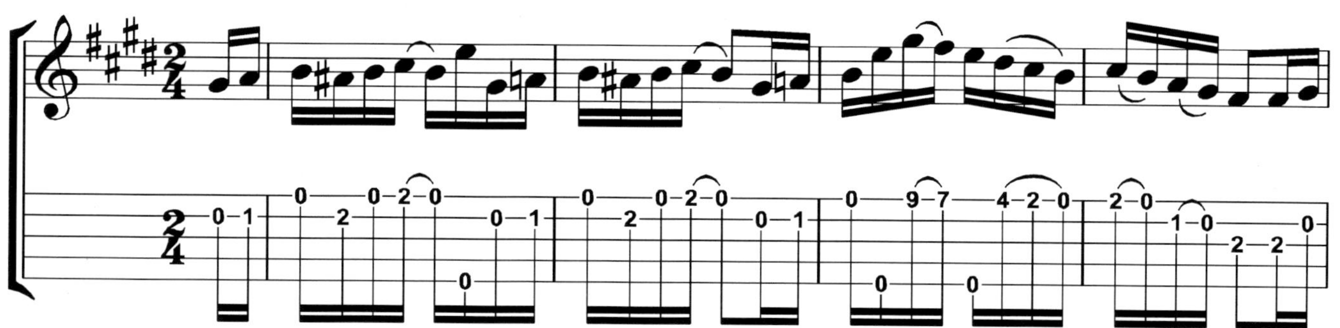

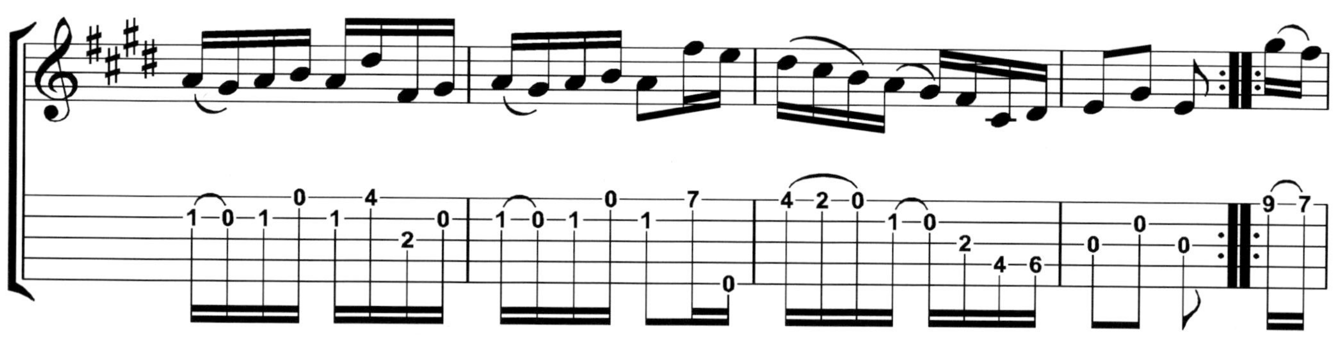

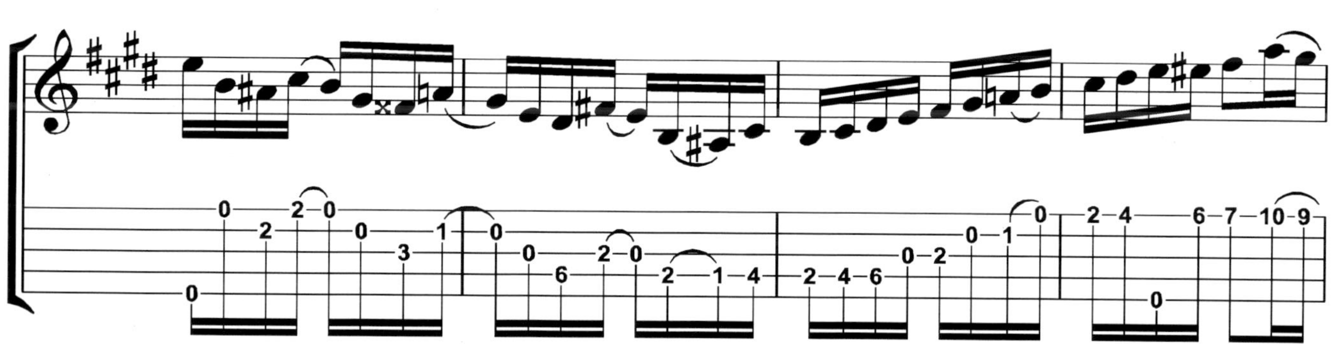

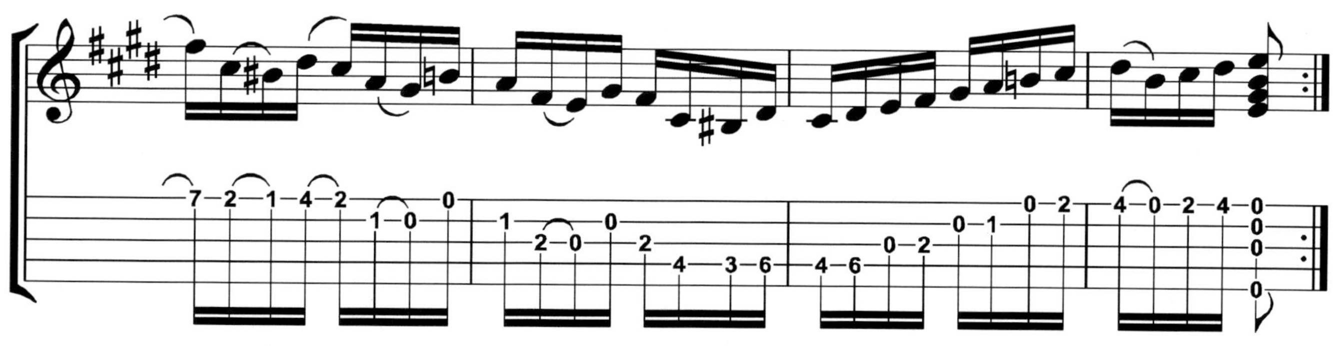

7
7. McCormick Party Reel
High 4th

8. Hard Back Family Reel

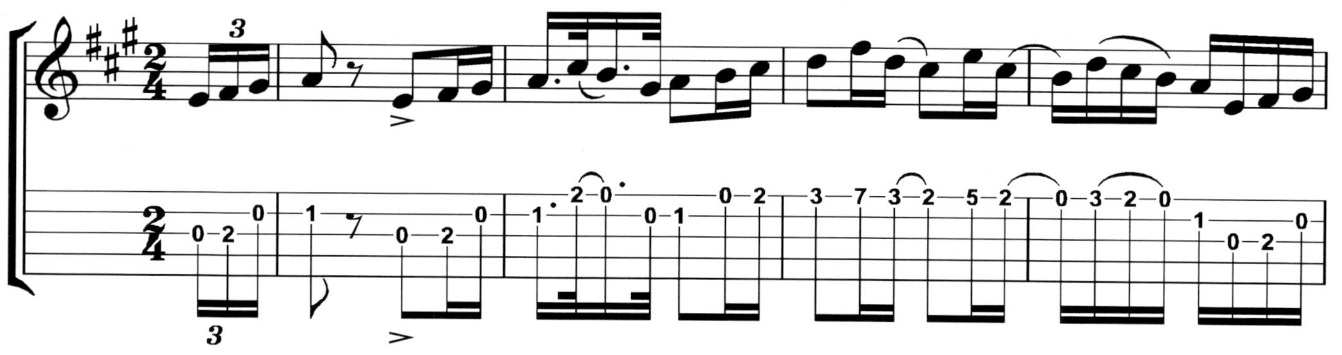

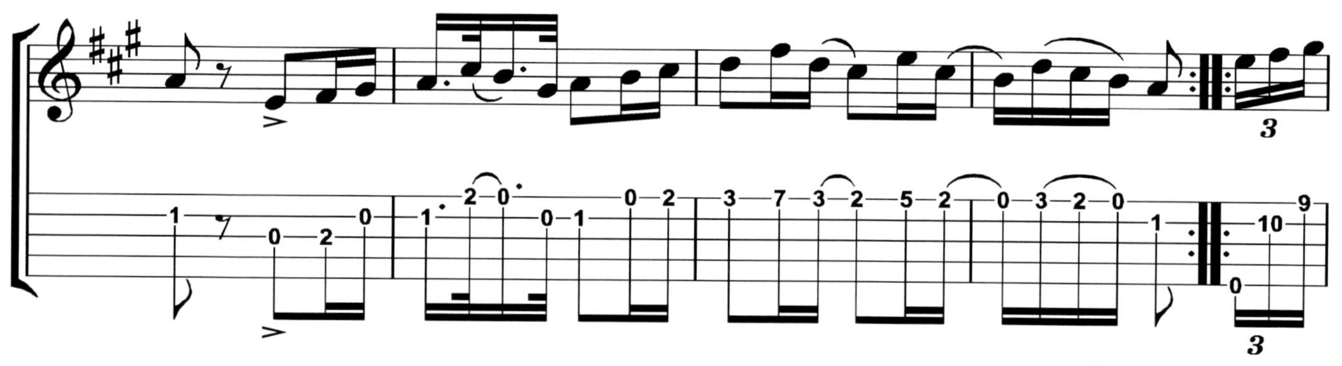

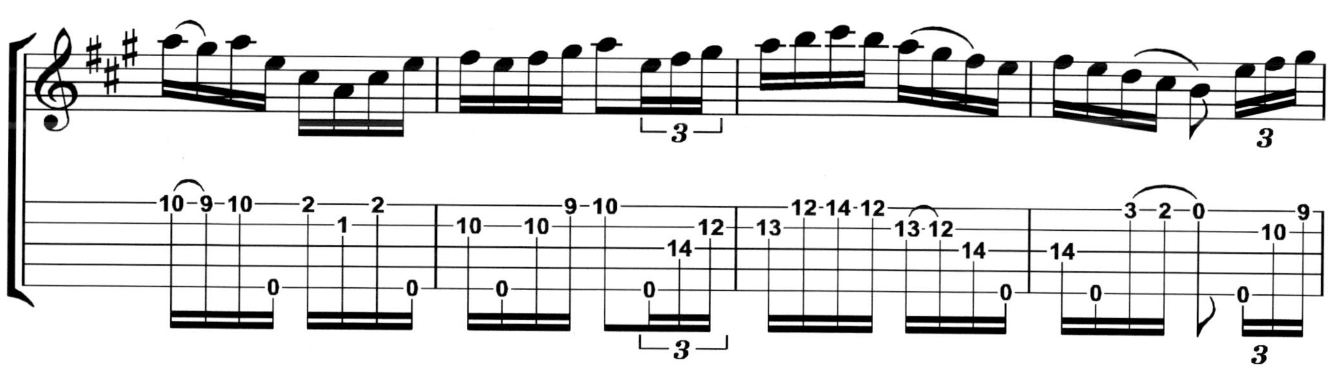

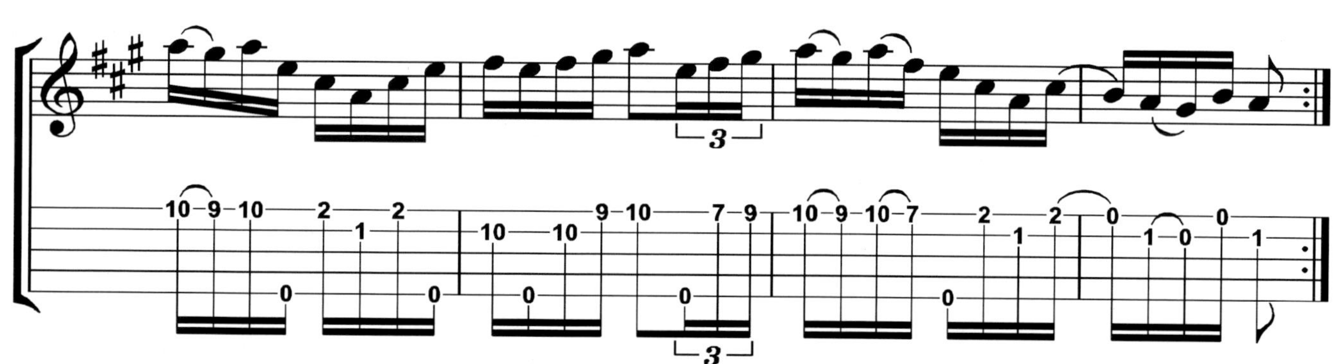

9. The Boss Reel

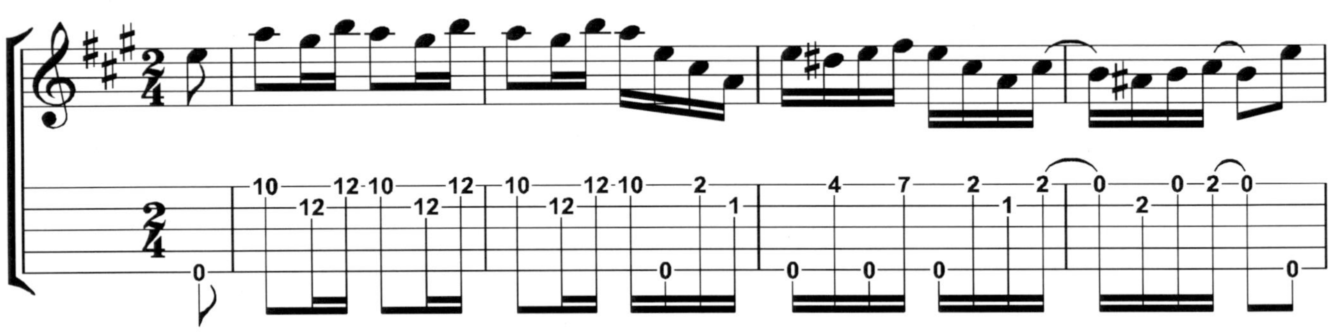

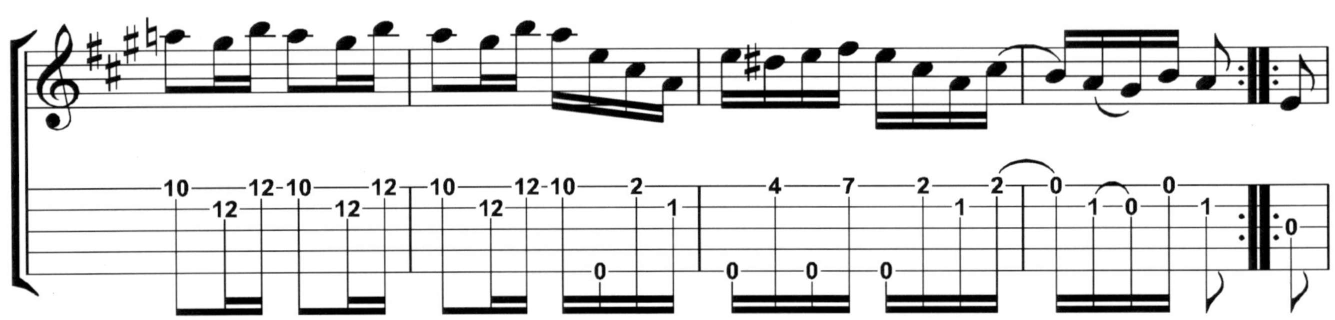

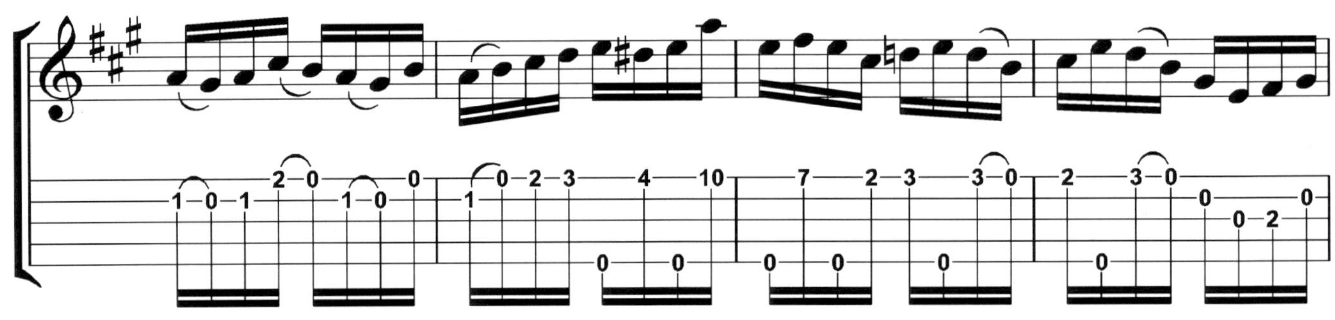

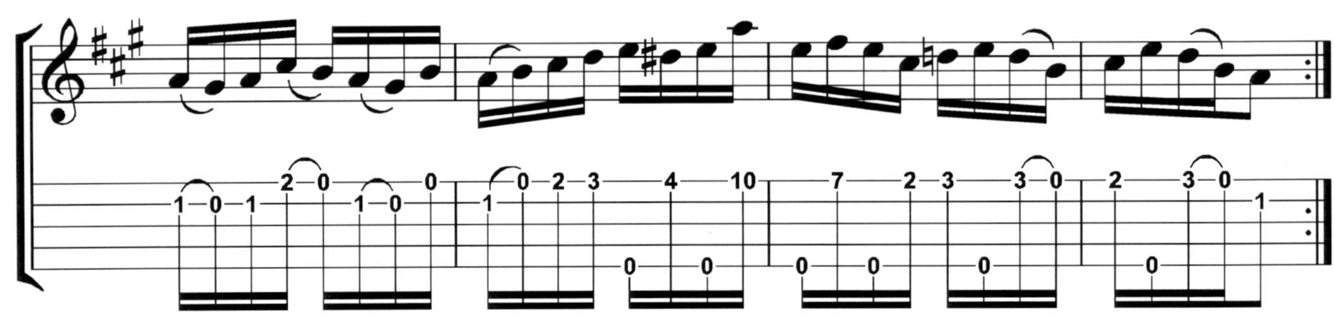

10. Trouble Begins Reel

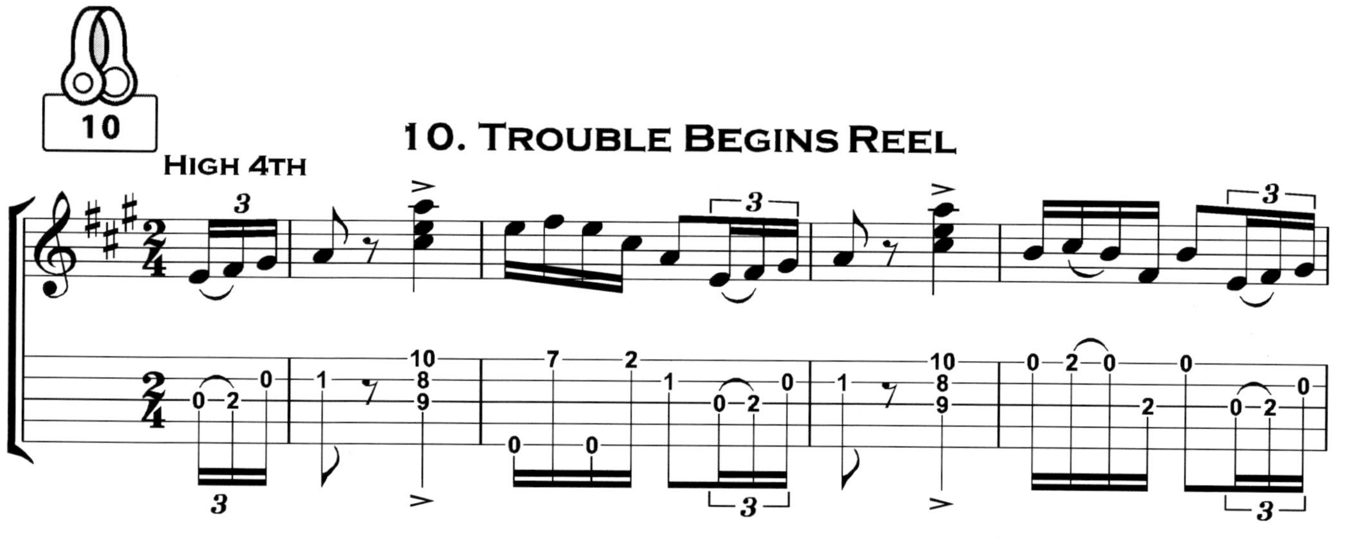

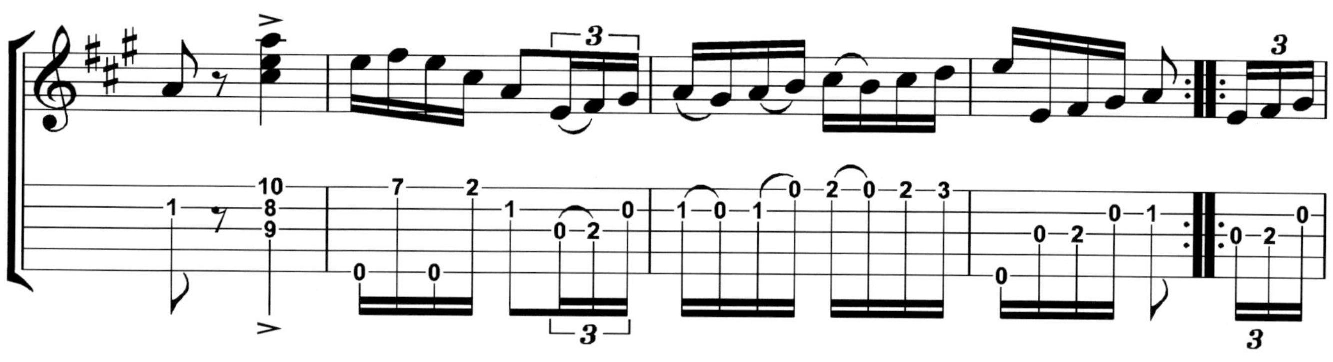

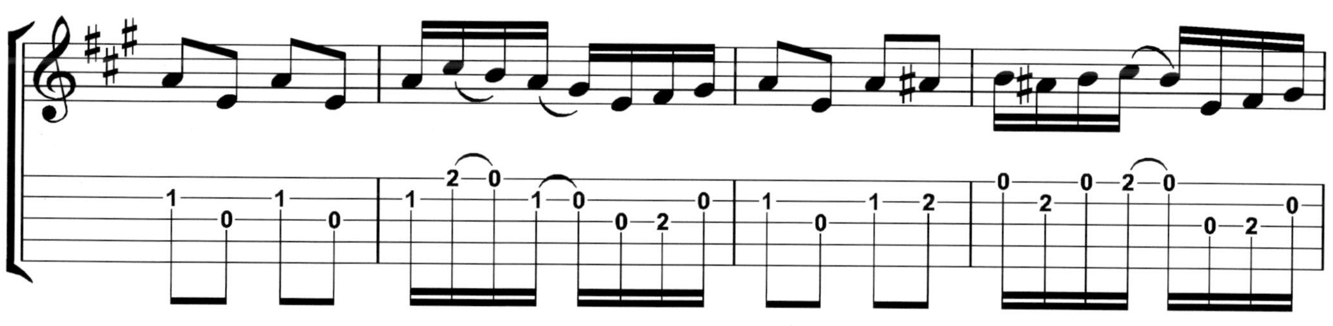

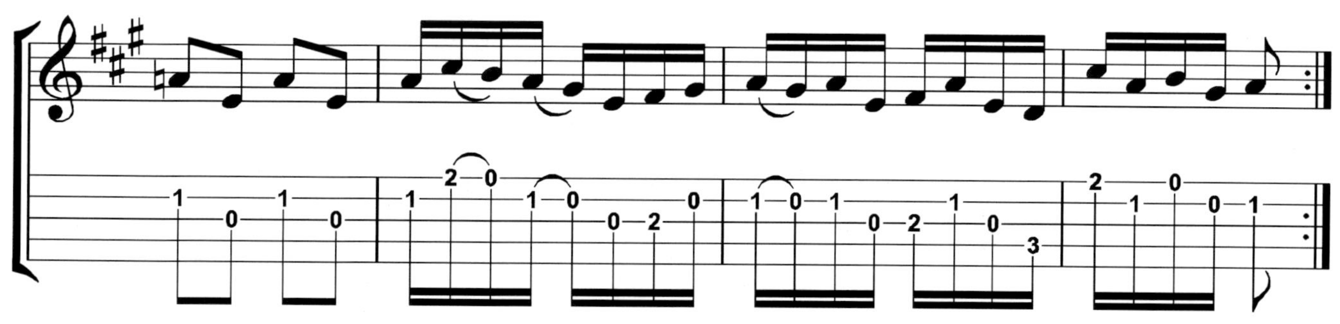

11

11. The Pic-Nic Reel

High 4th

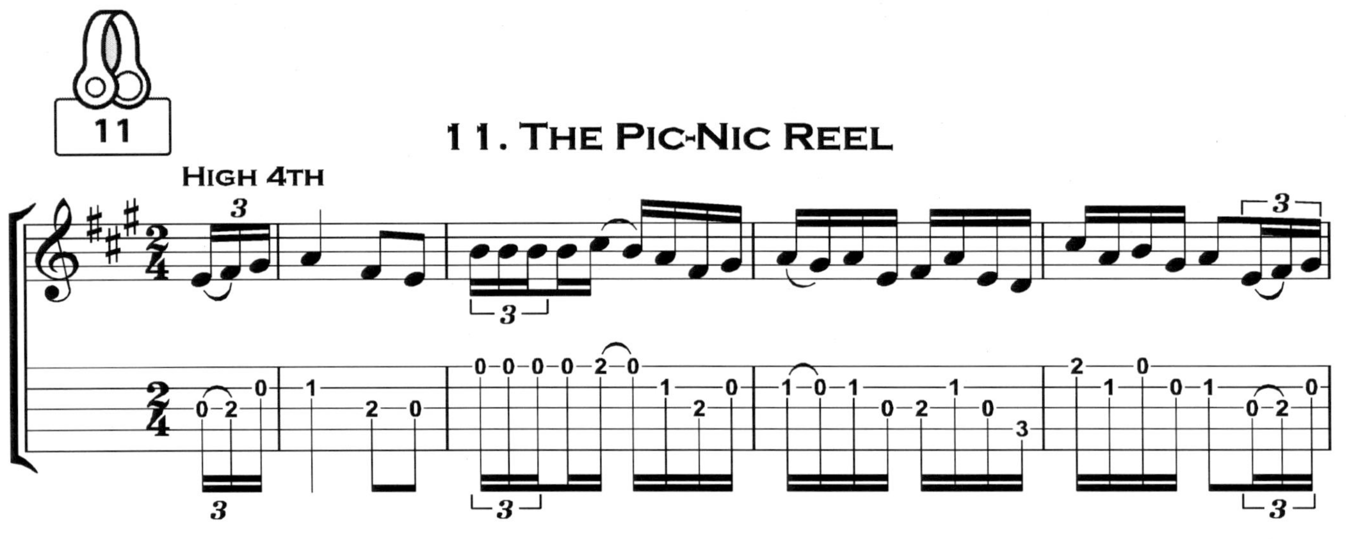

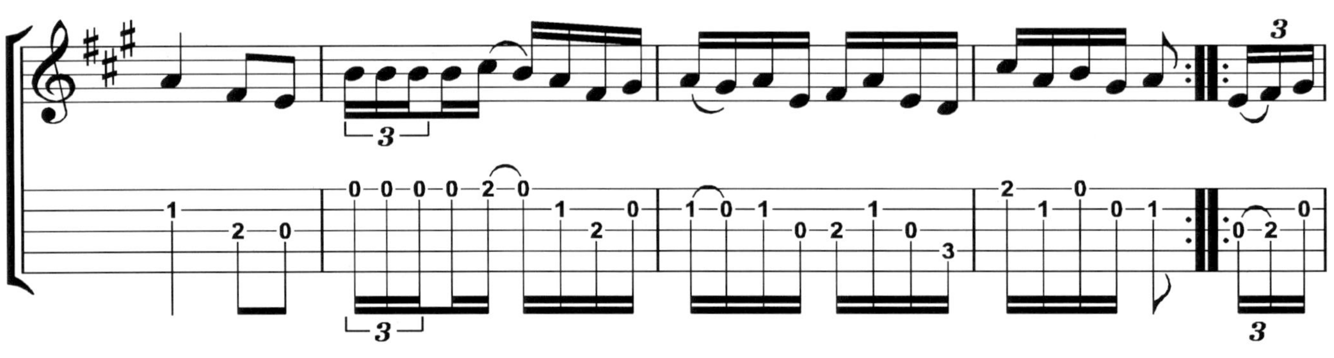

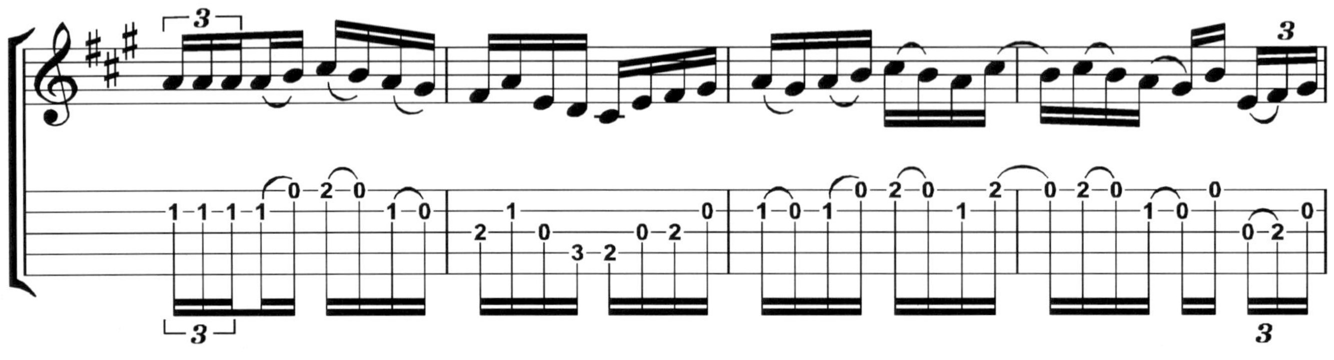

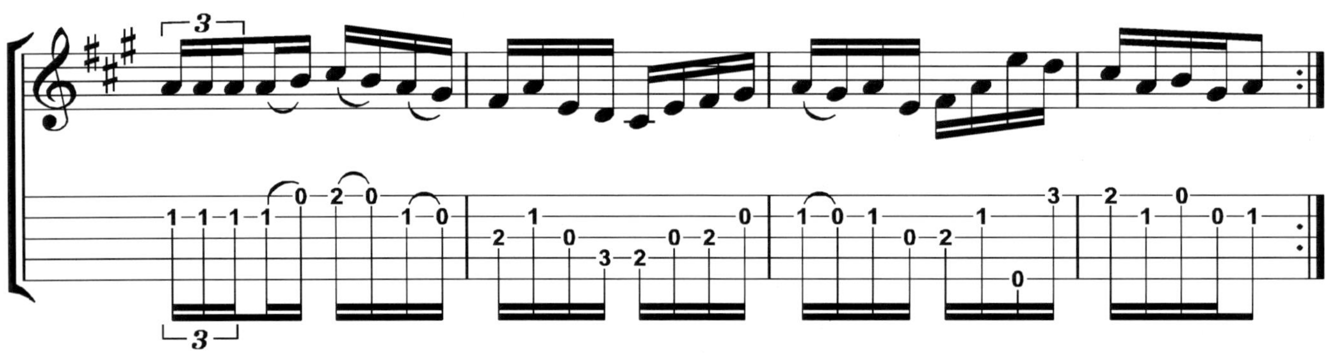

12. All Night Reel

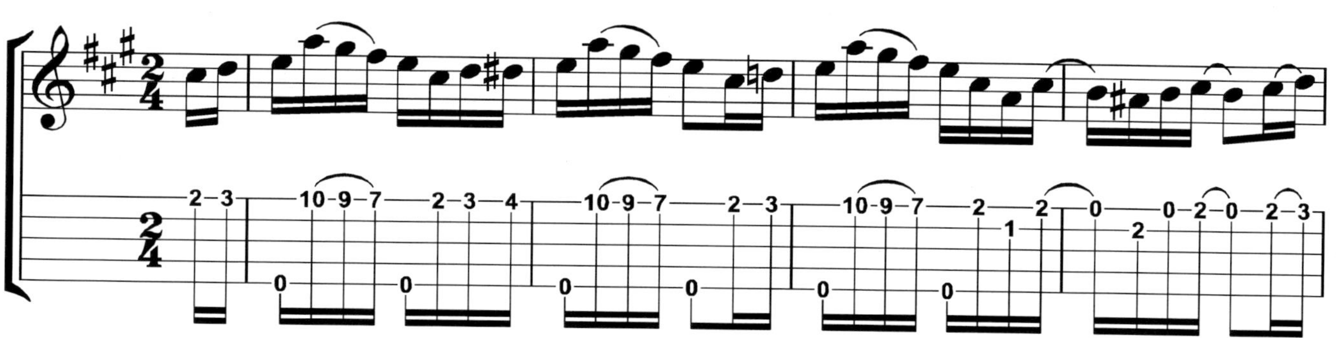

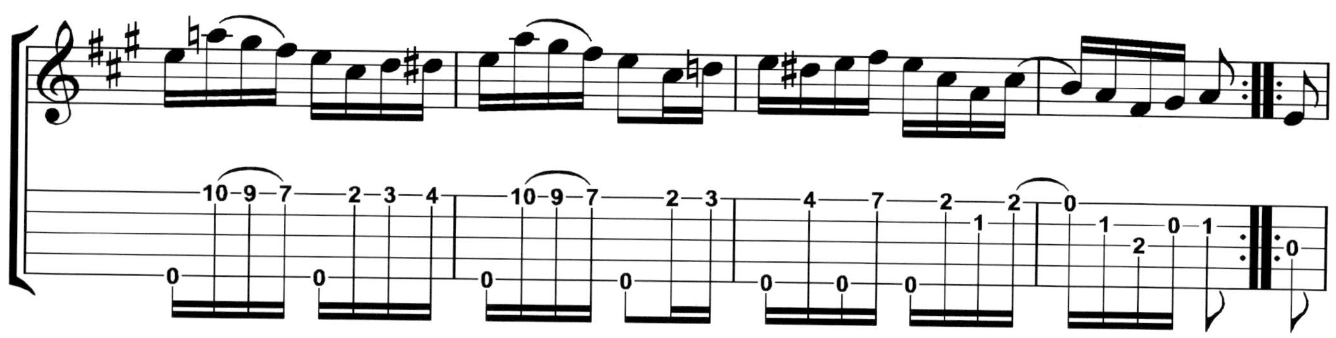

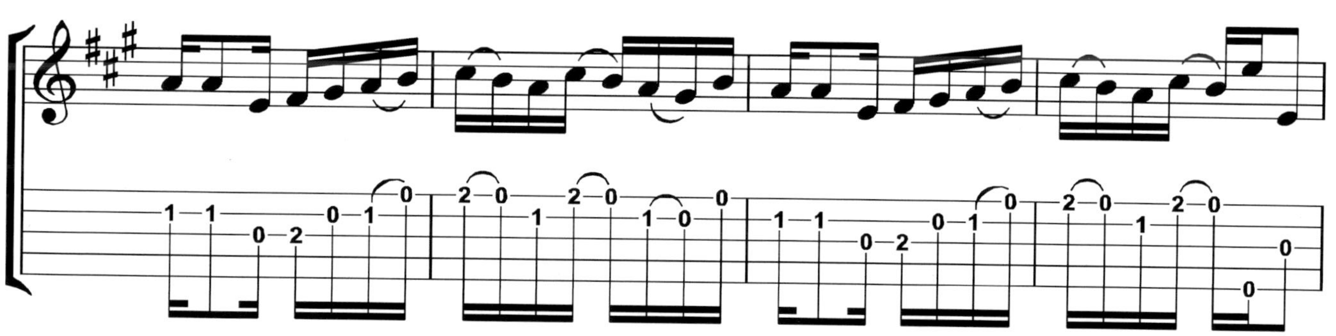

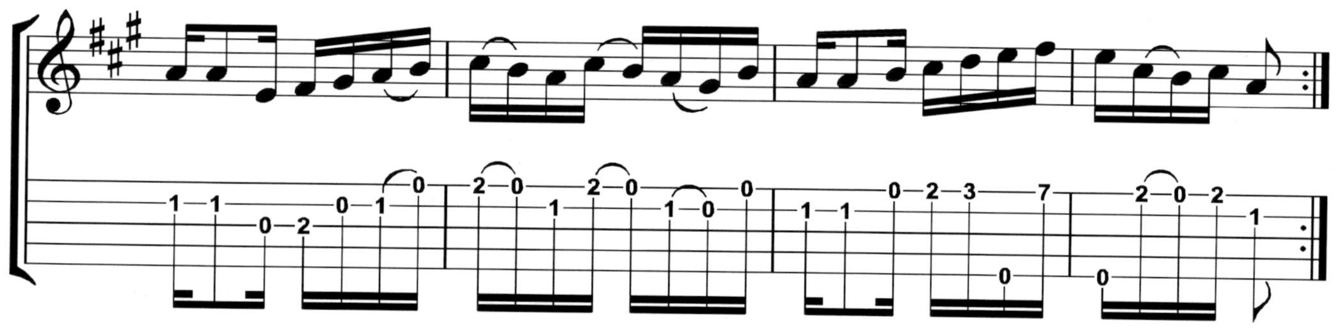

13. Always Happy Reel

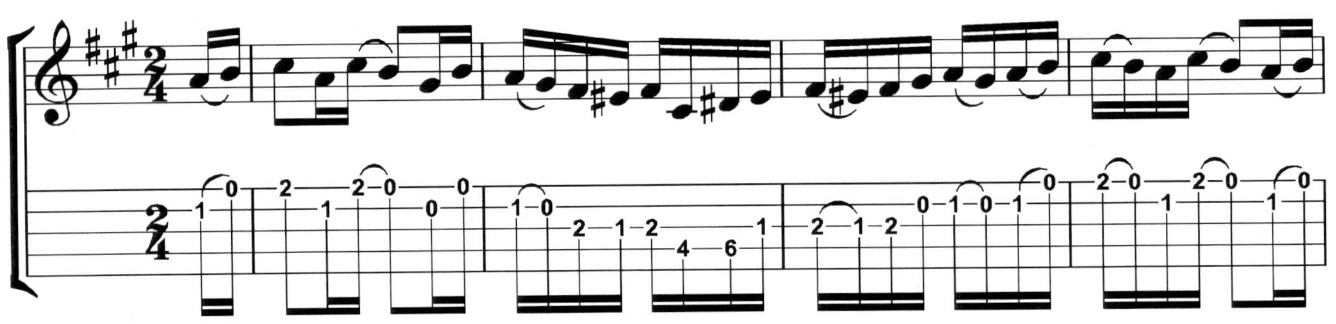

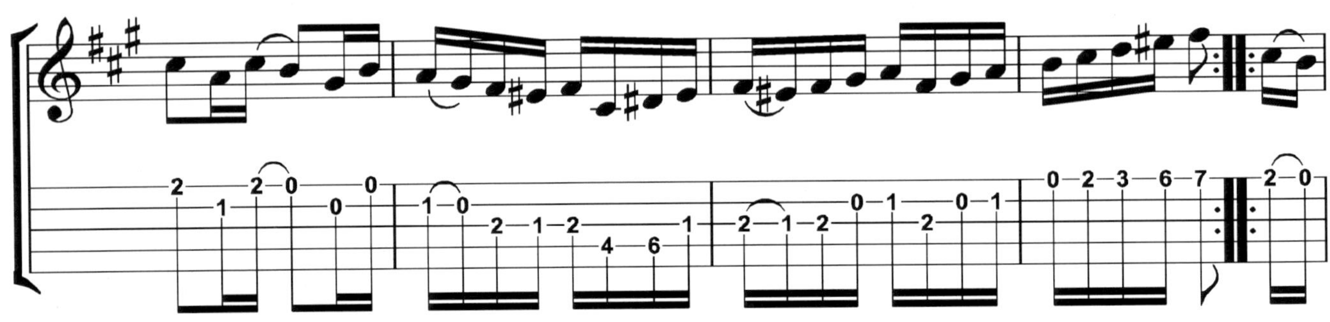

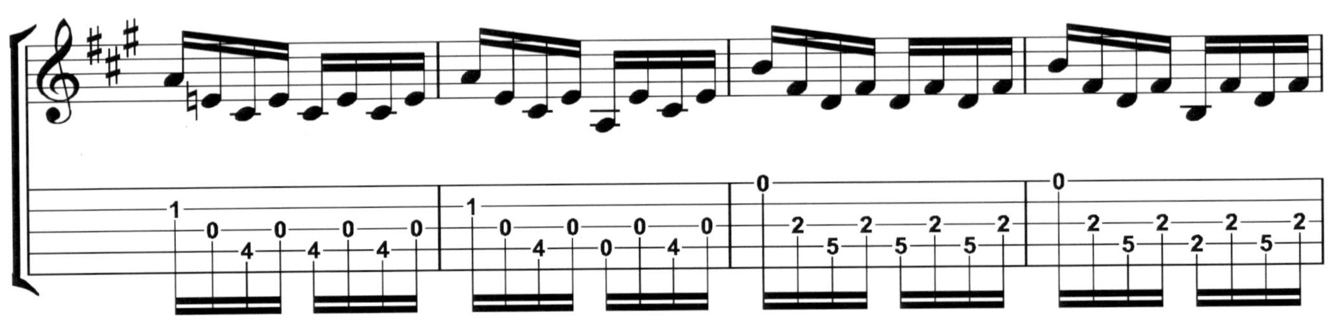

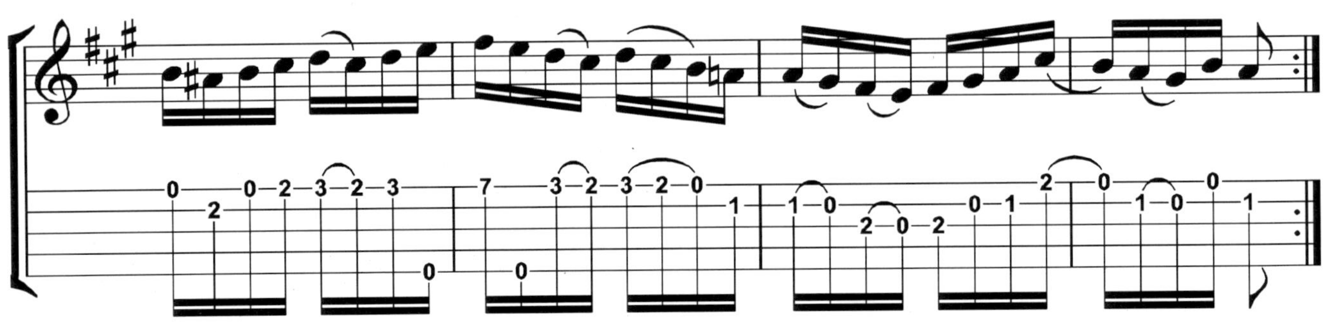

14. Sir Joseph Hornpipe

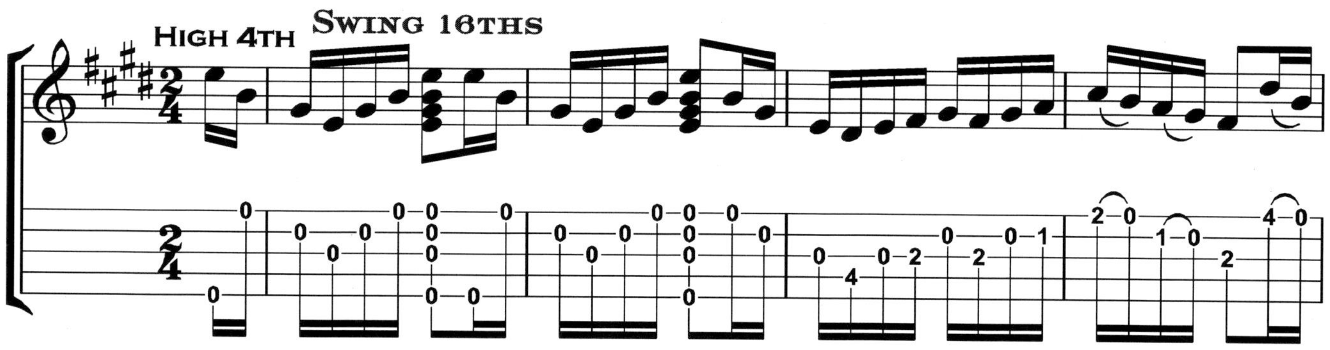

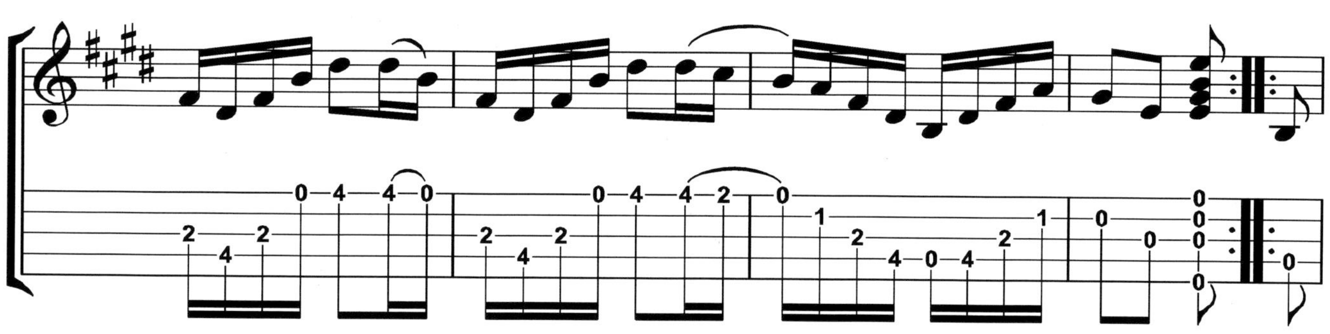

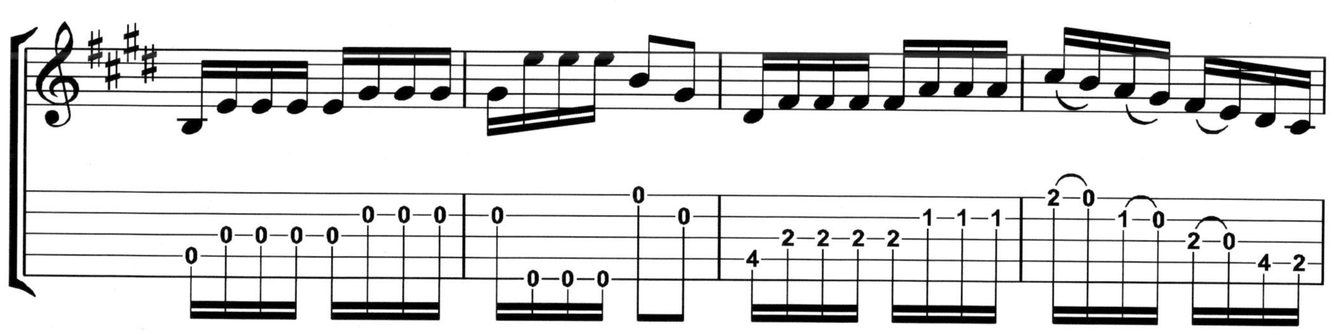

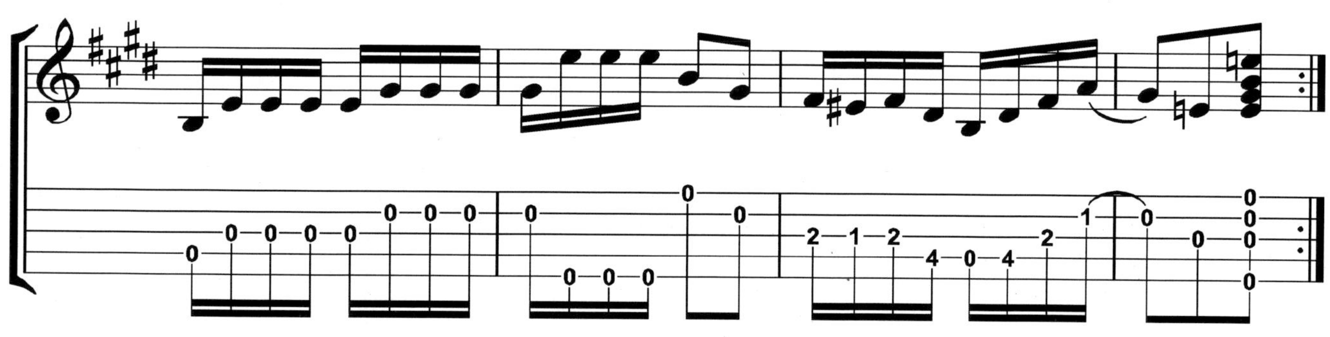

15. Good Enough Irish Reel

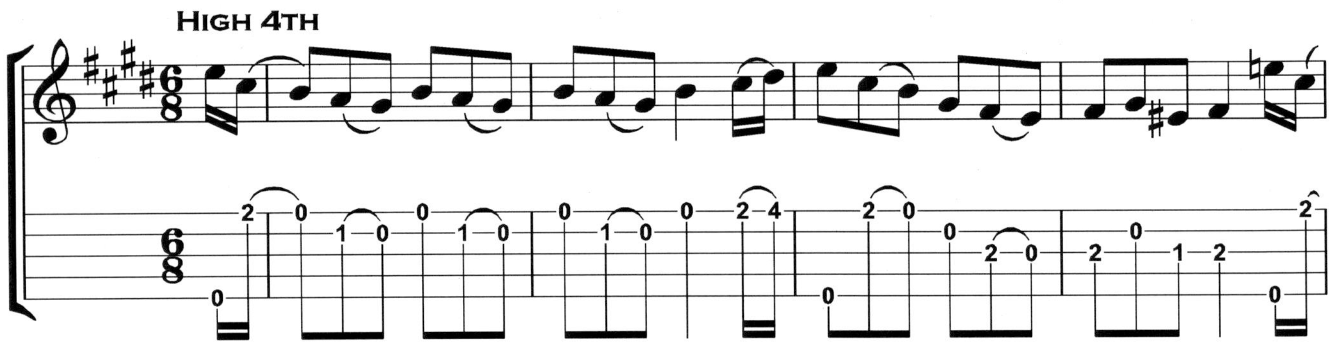

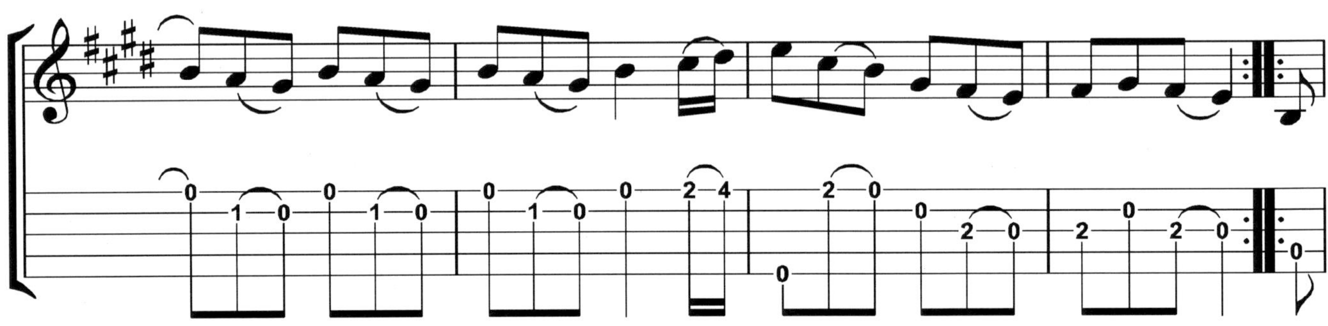

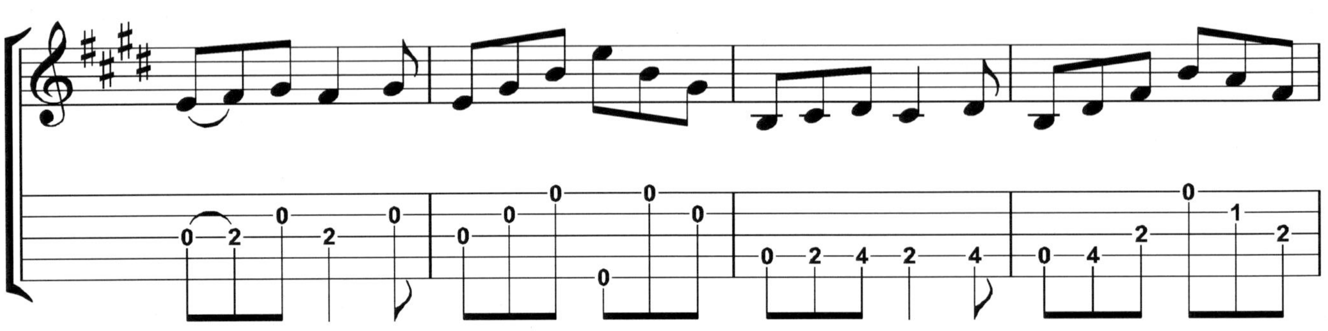

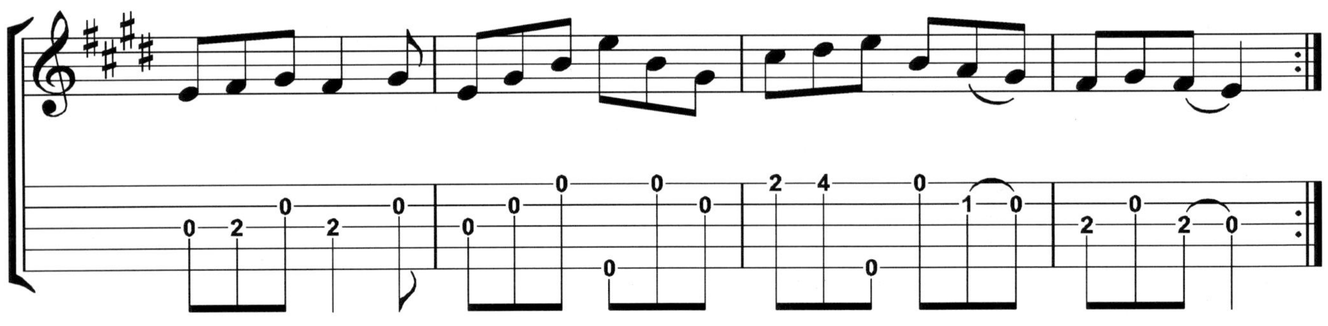

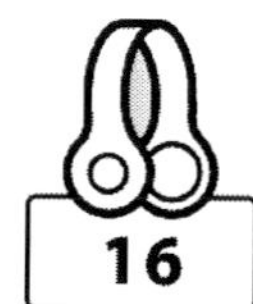

16. Before the Mast Hornpipe

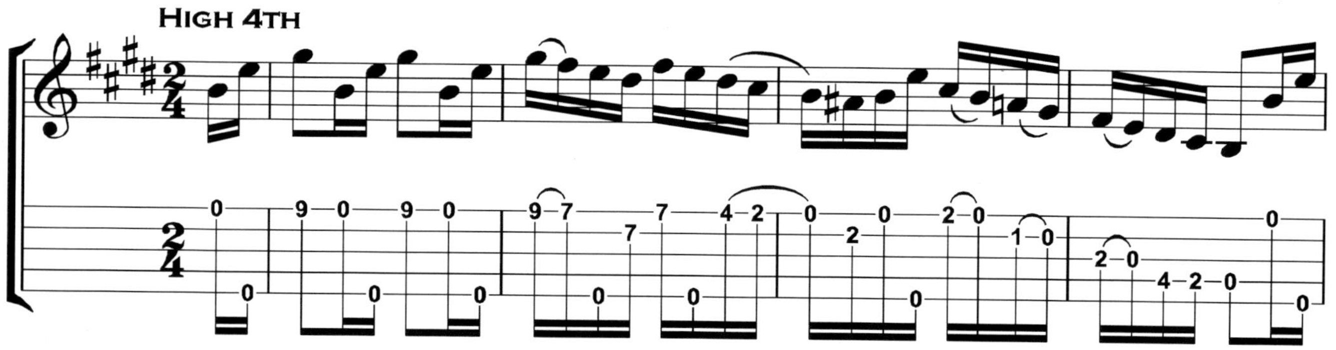

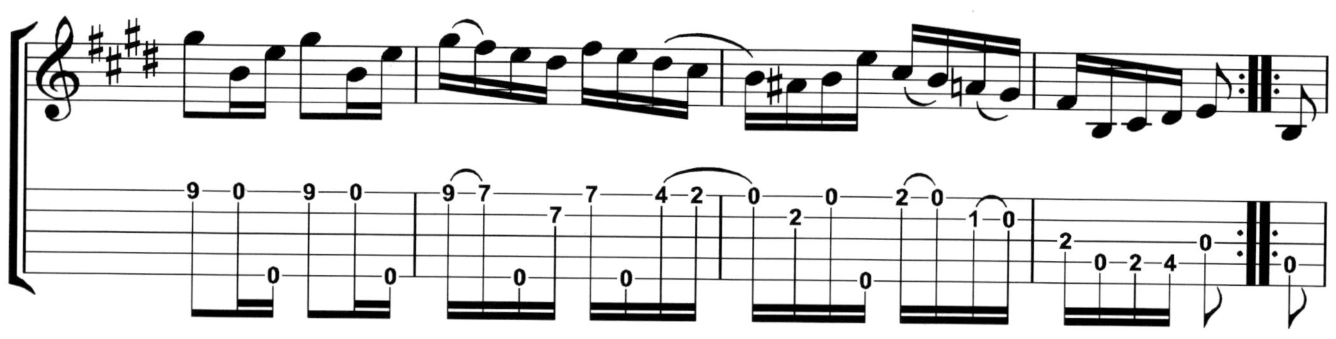

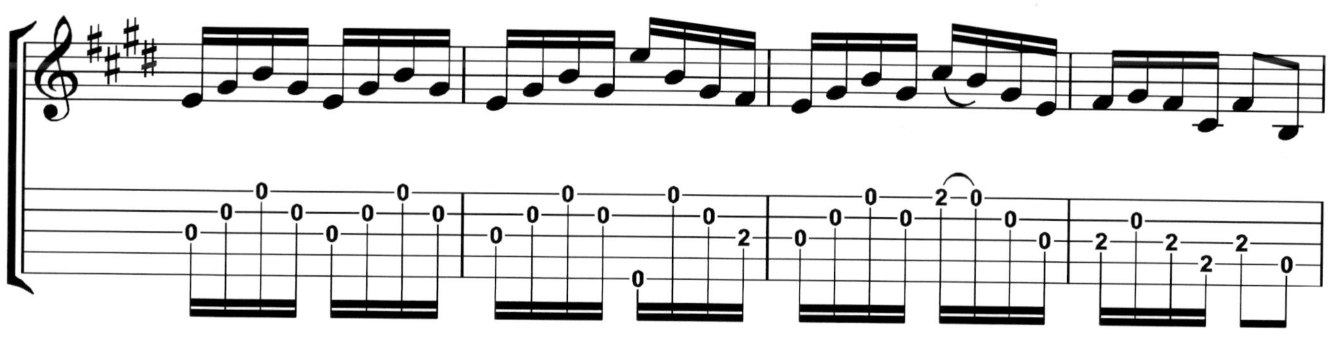

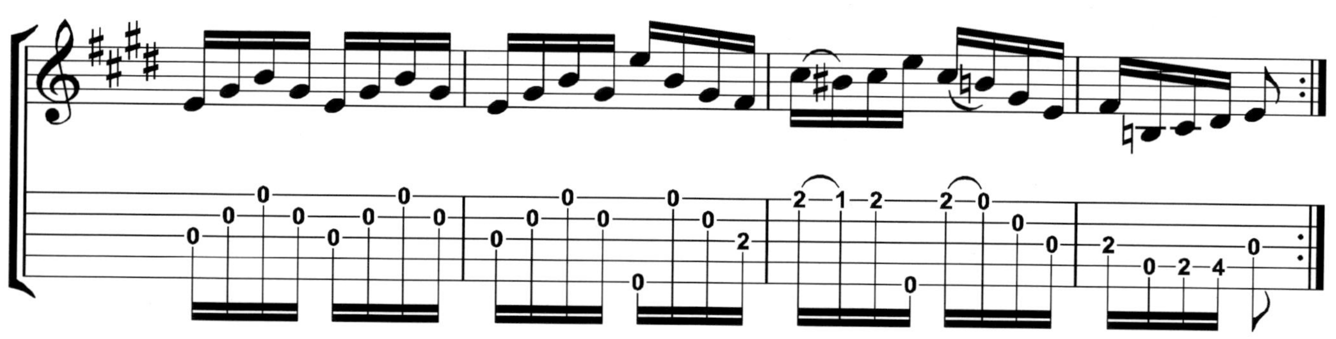

17. Mary McCarty Irish Reel

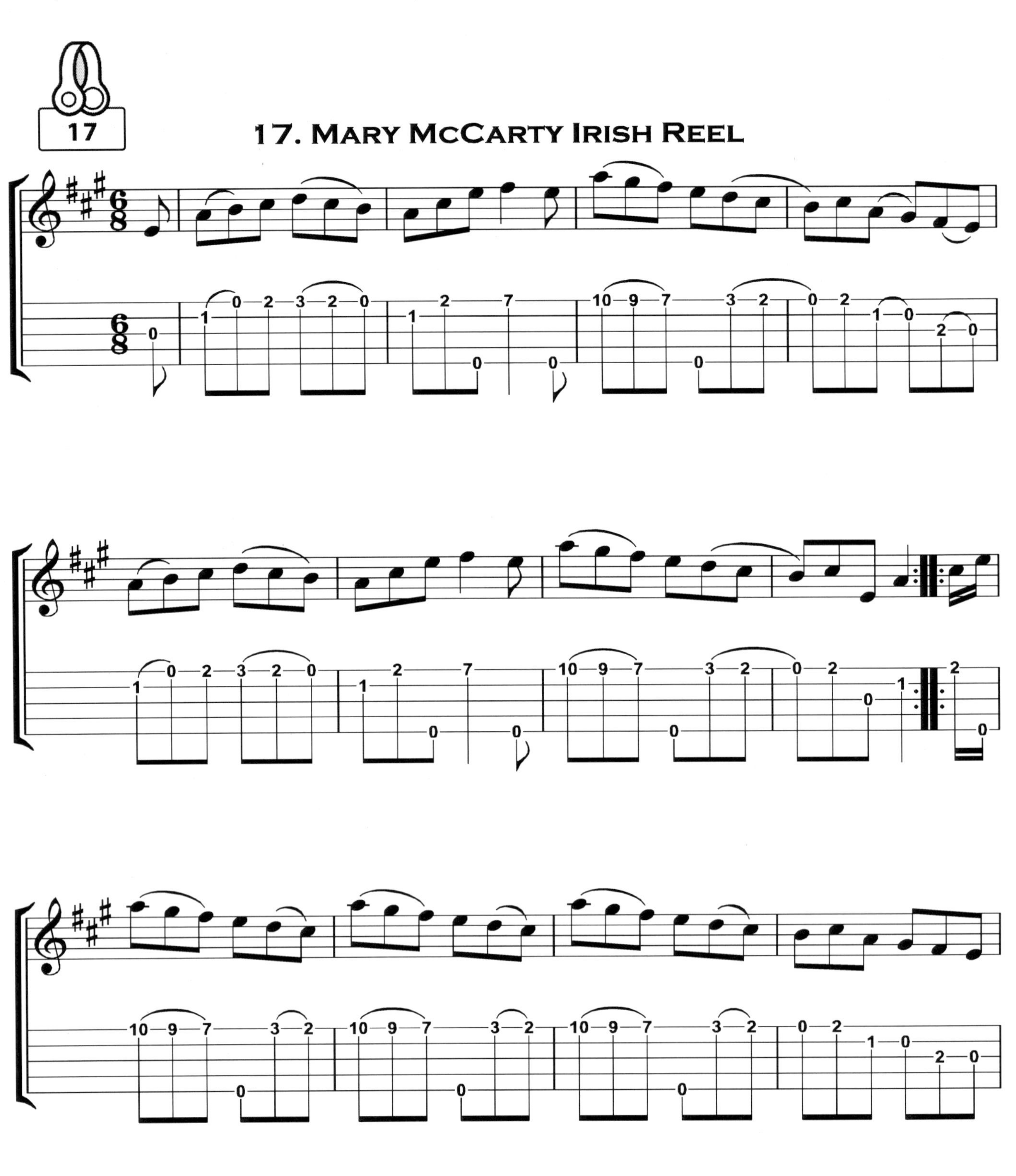

18. Latest Racket Reel

High 4th

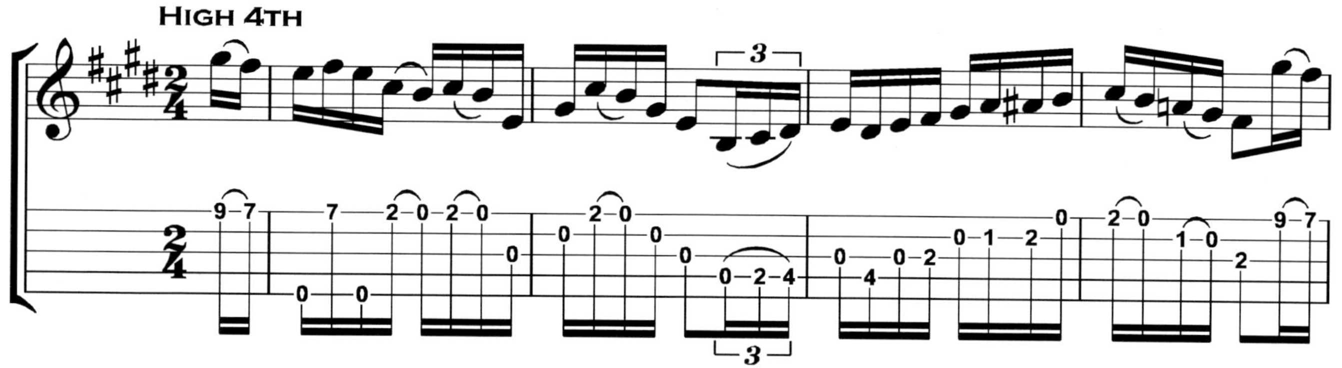

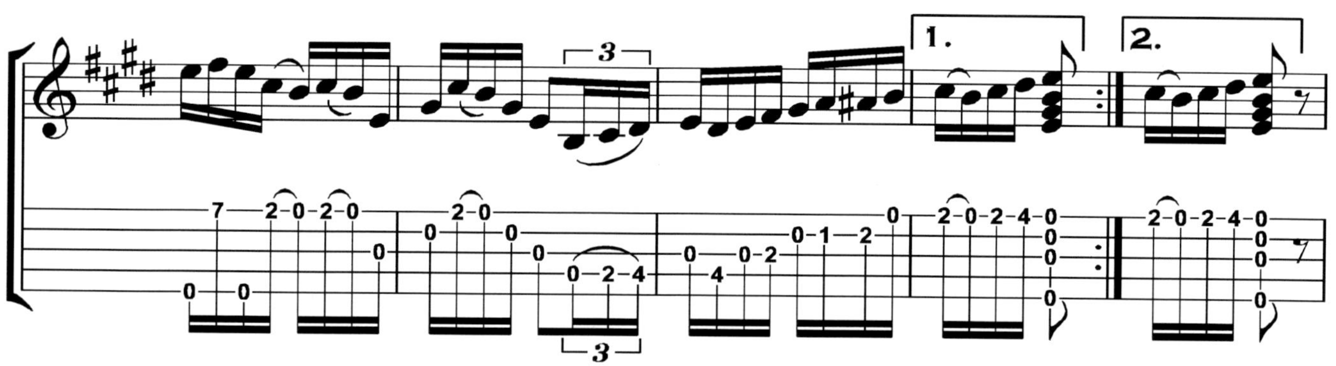

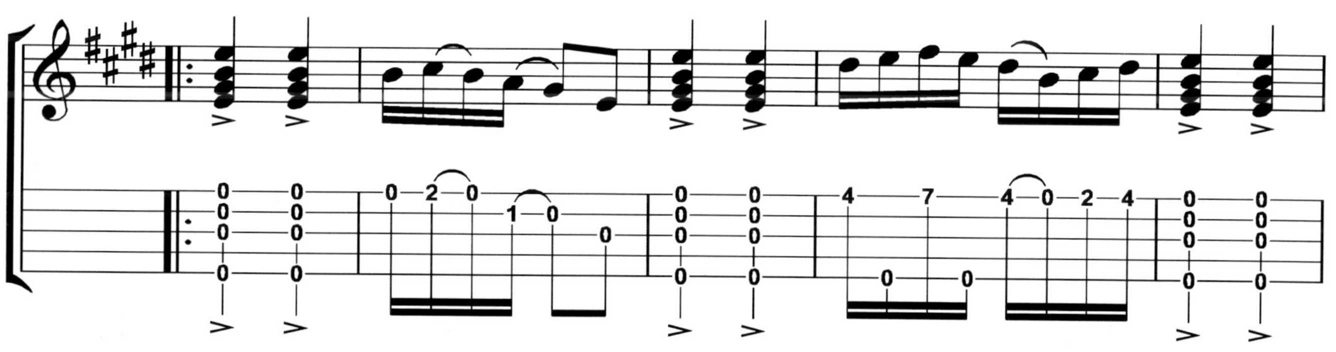

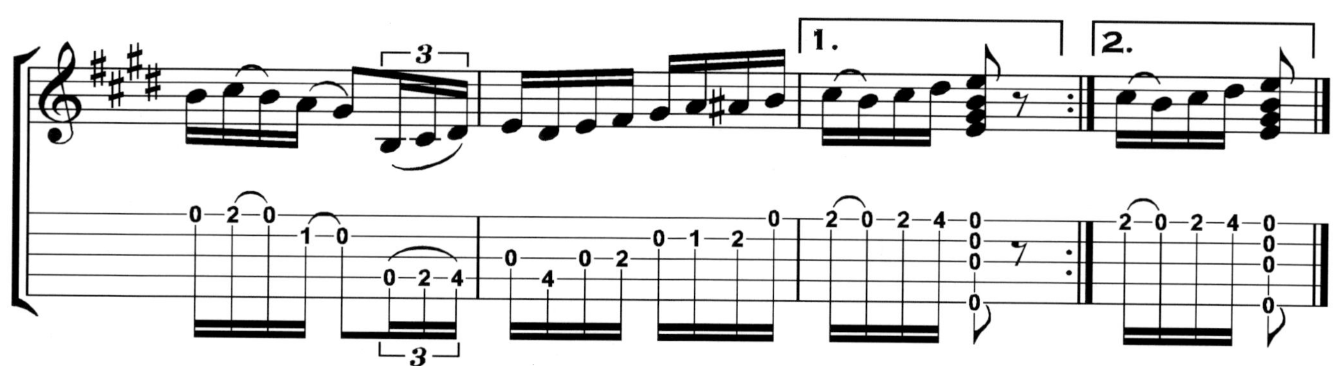

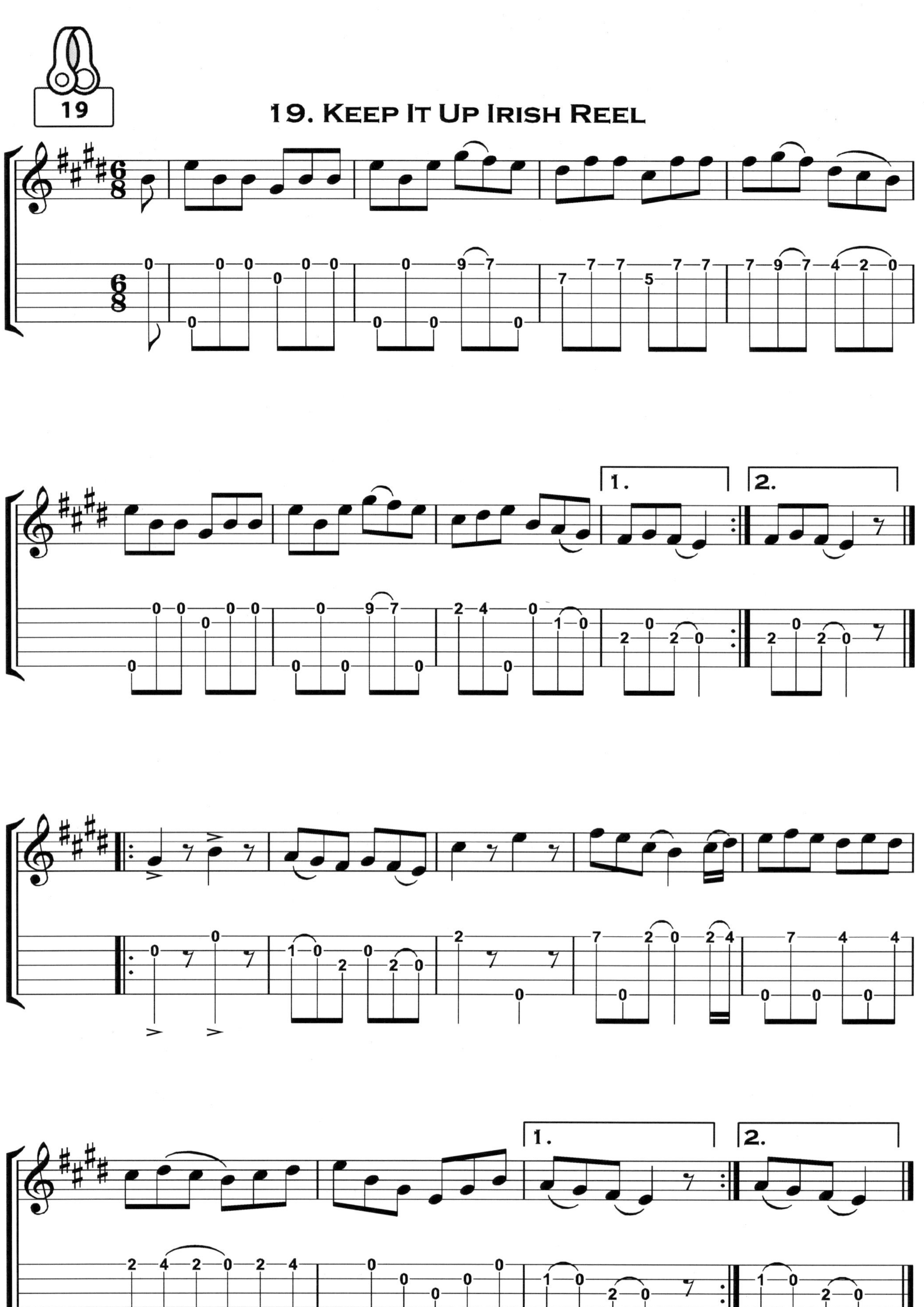
19
19. Keep It Up Irish Reel
1.
2.
1.
2.

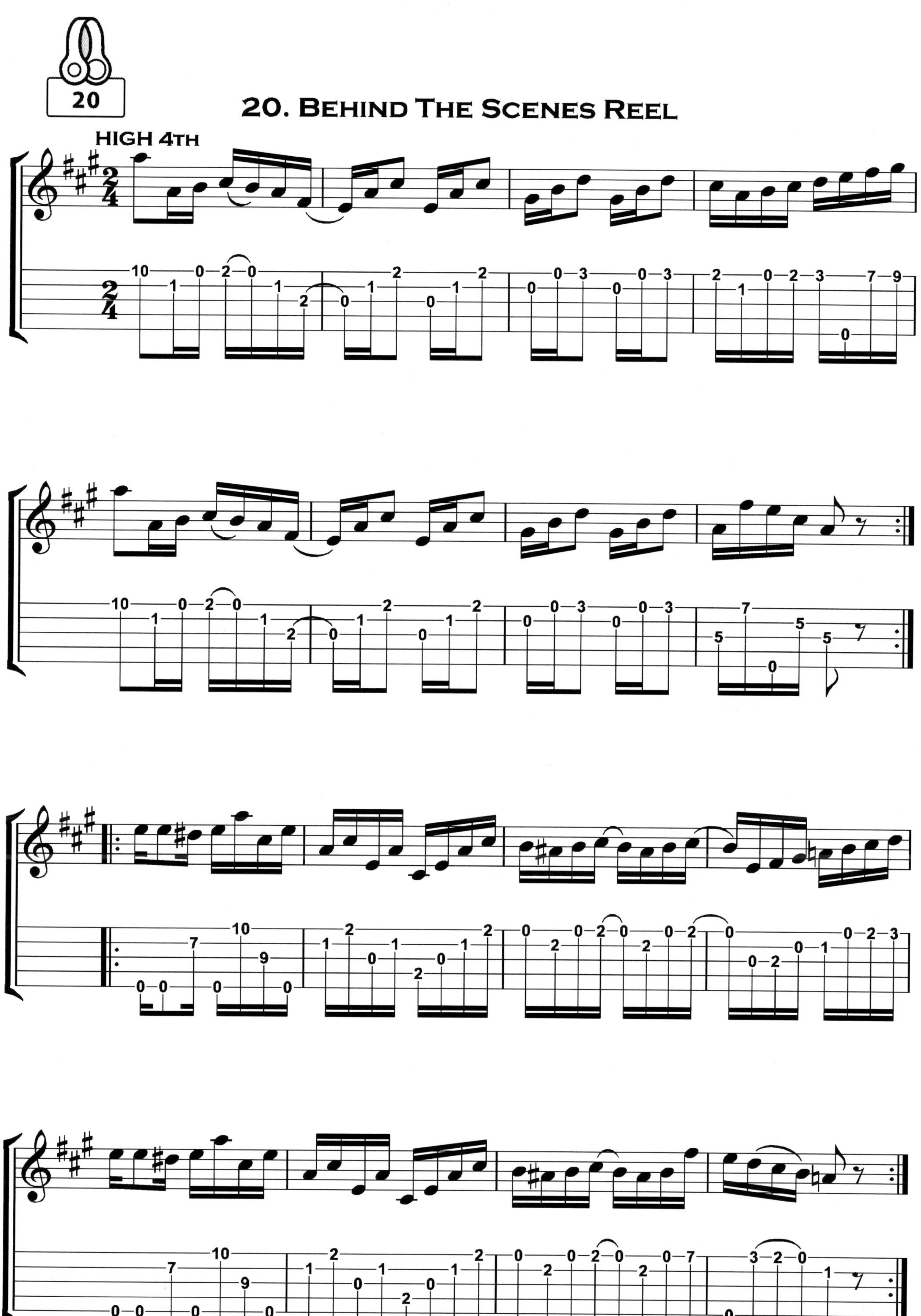
20
20. Behind The Scenes Reel
HIGH 4TH

21. Rooney's Favorite Irish Reel

HIGH 4TH

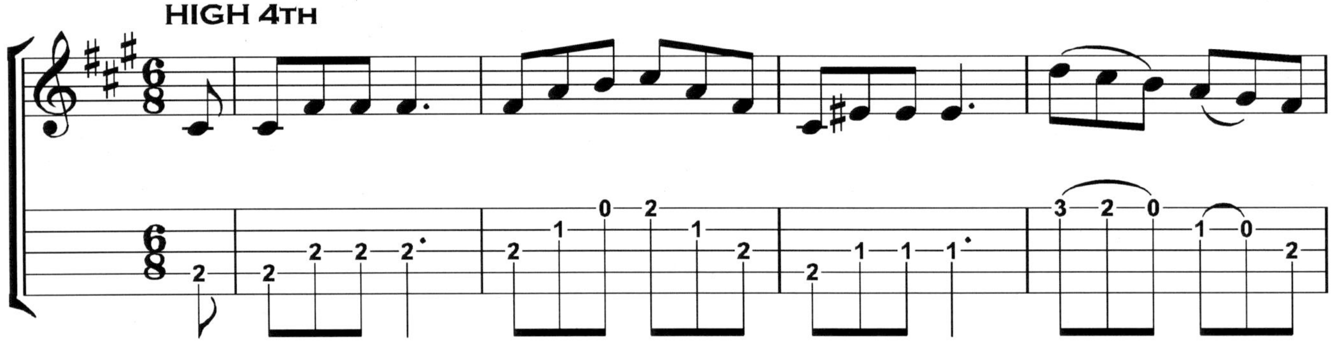

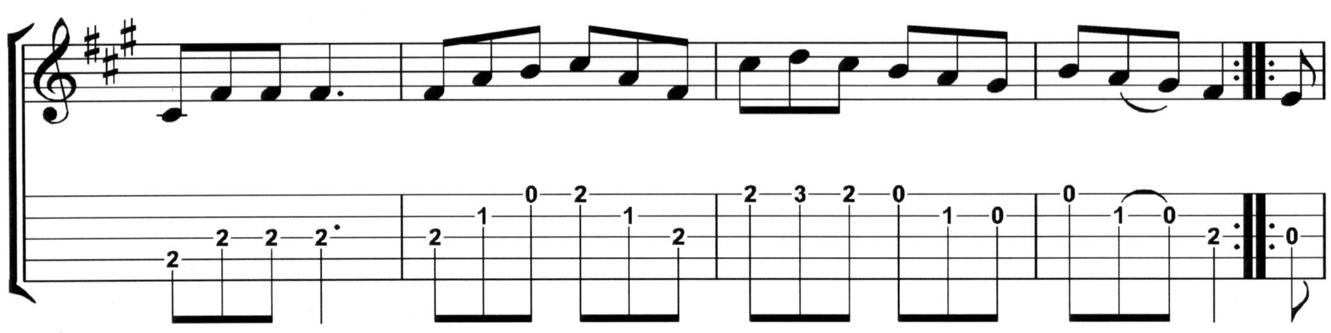

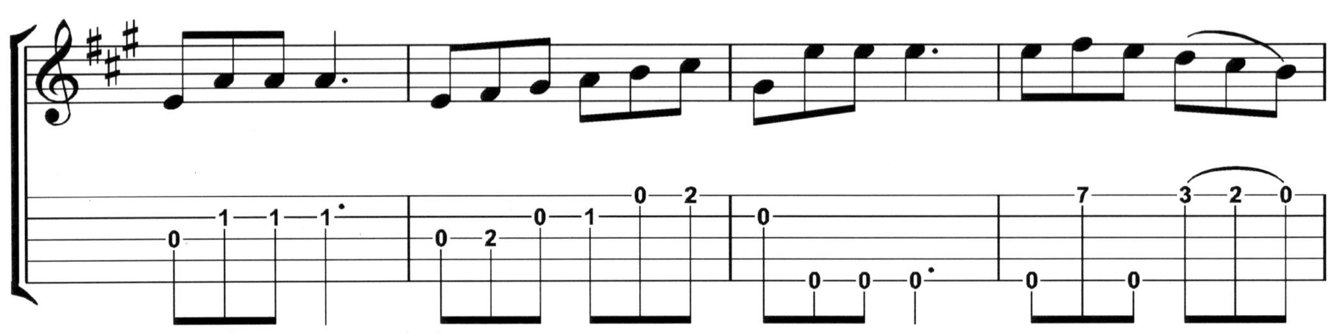

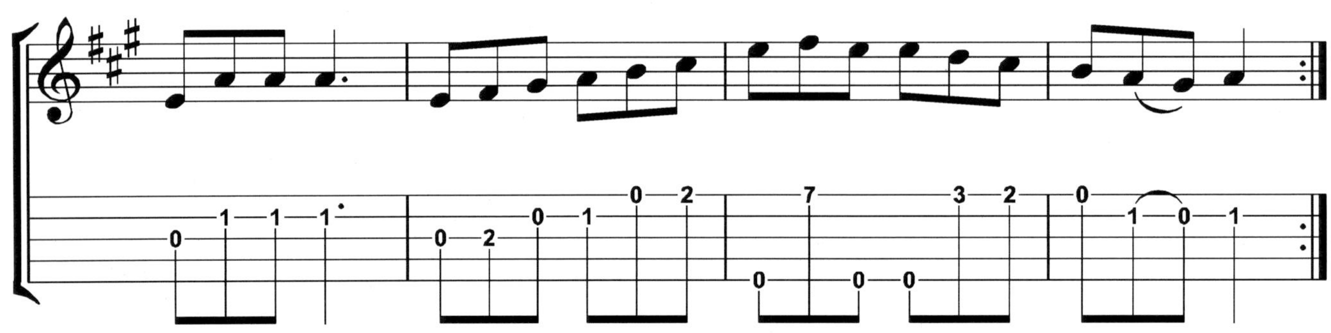

22. Lively Twins Reel

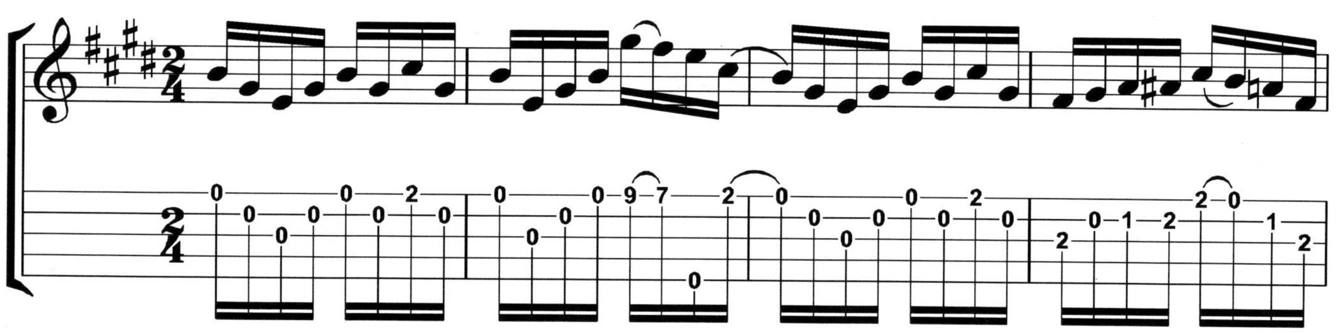

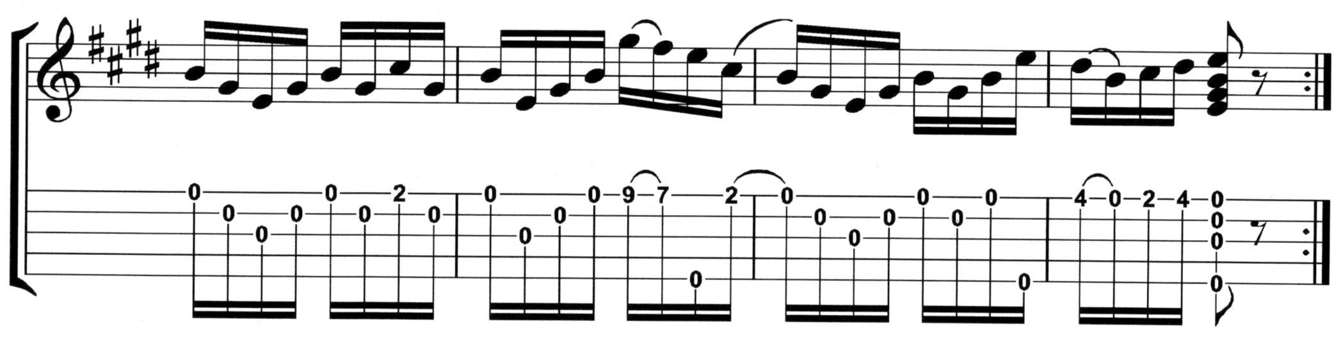

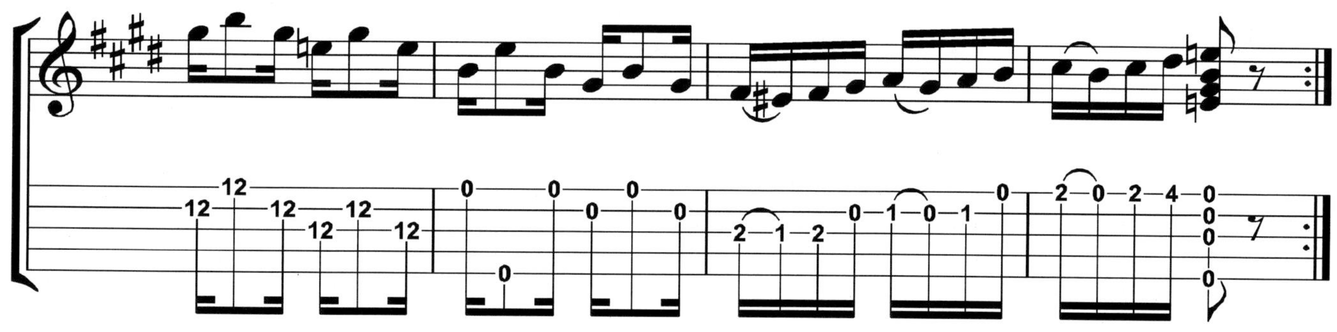

23. McGinley's Reel

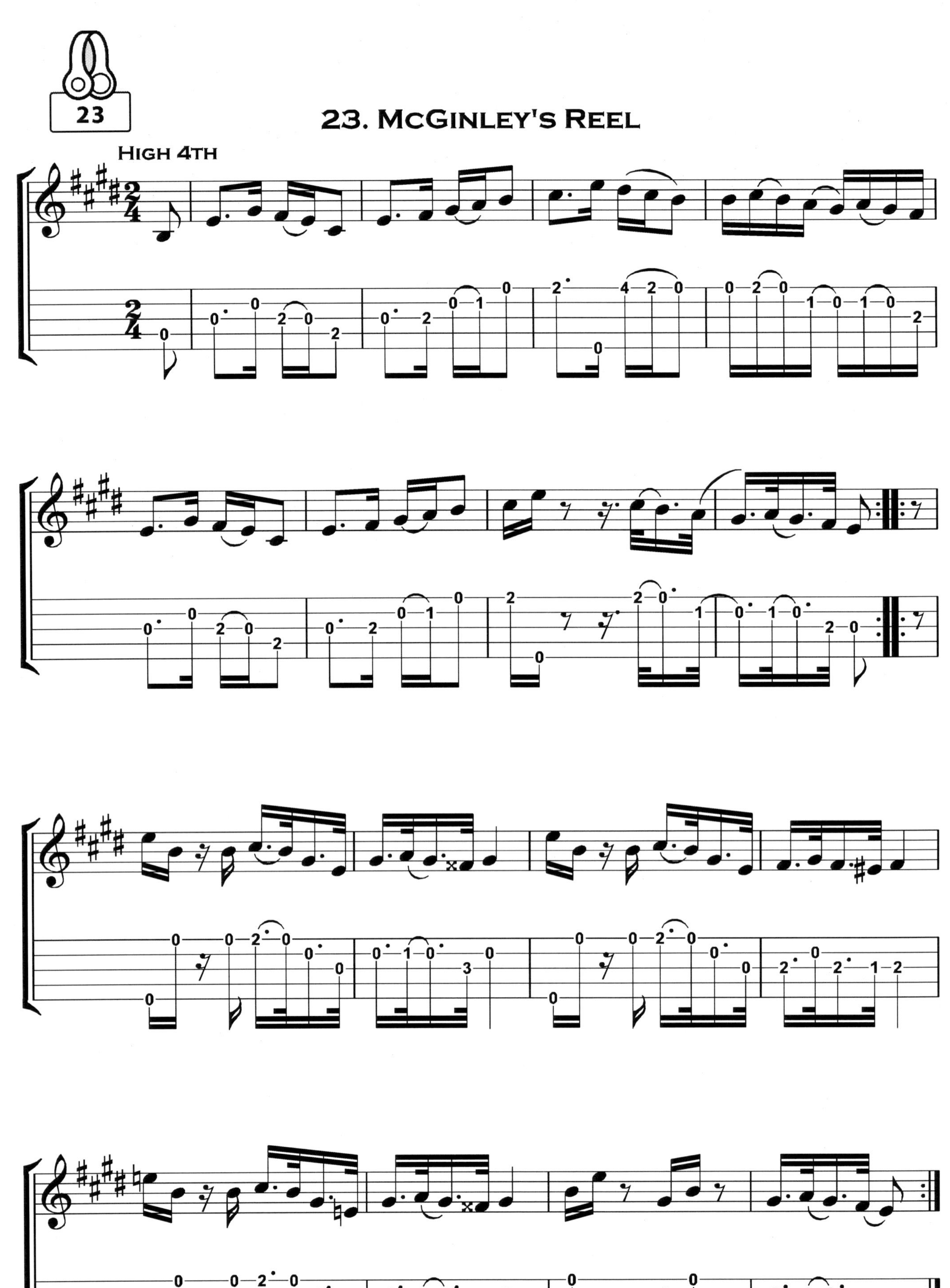

24. Dick Deadeye Hornpipe

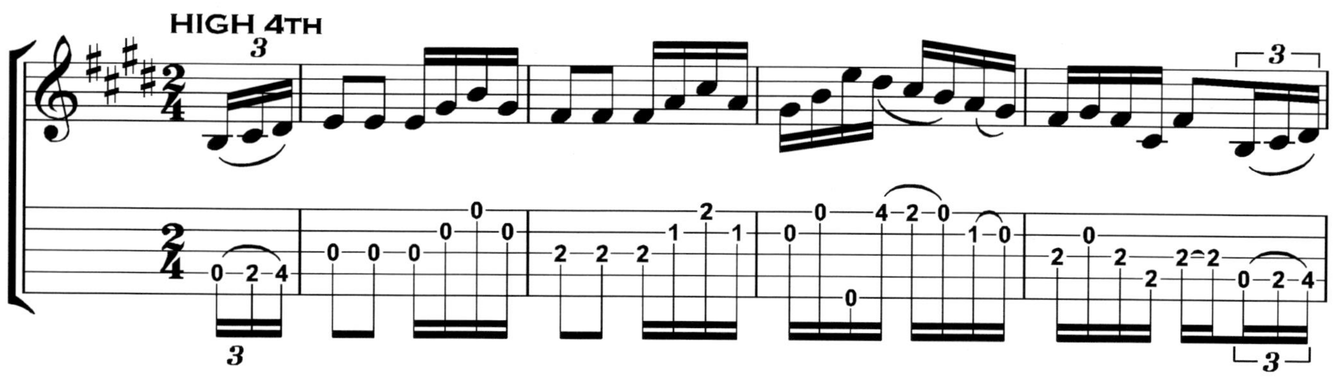

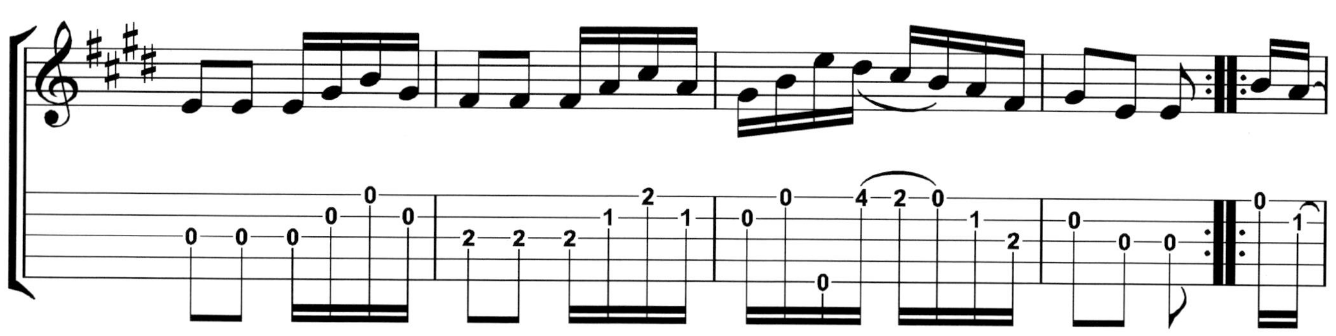

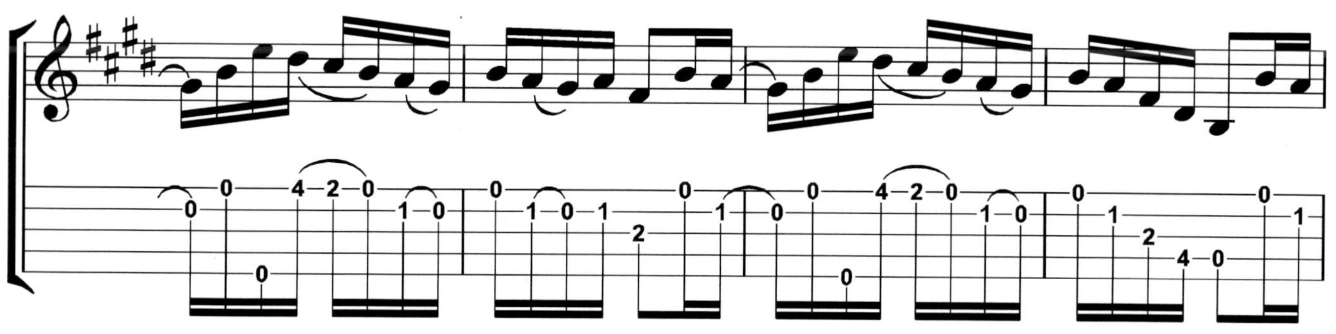

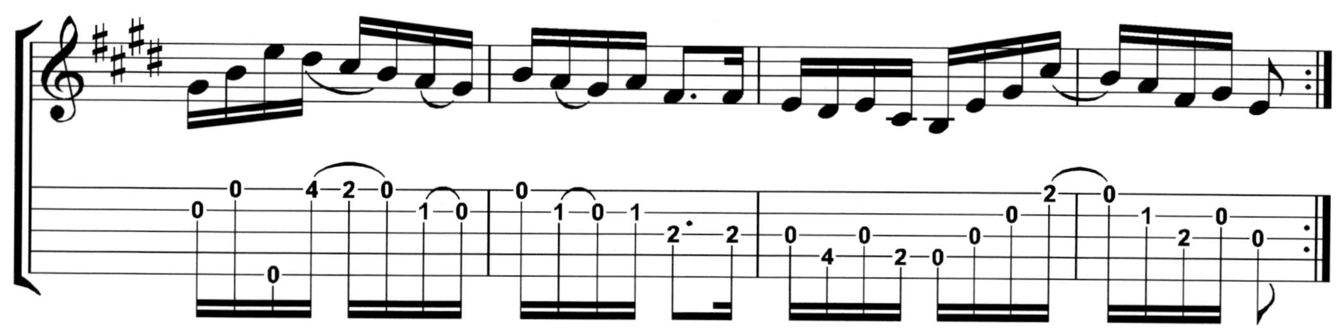

25. First Mate Hornpipe

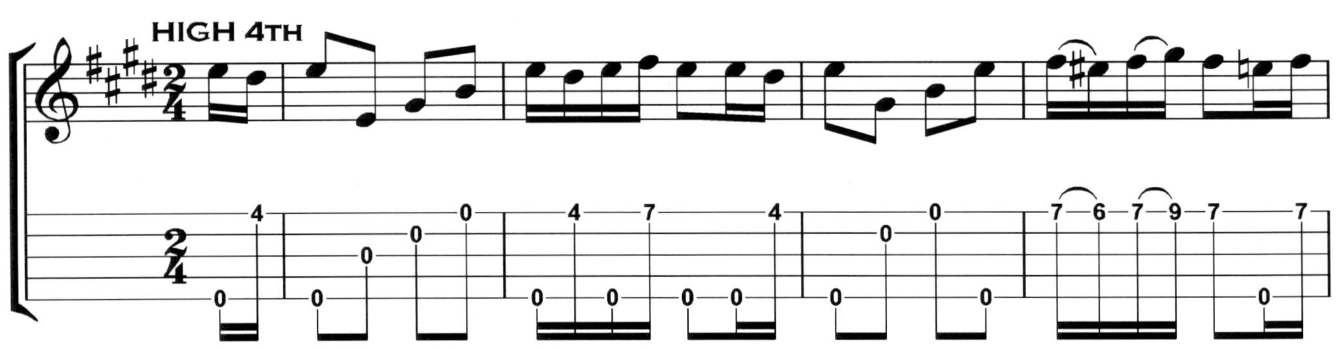

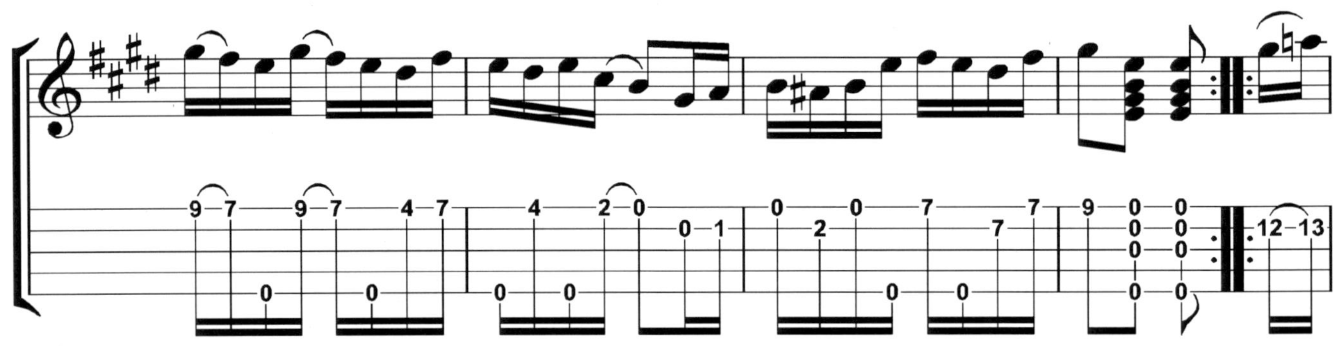

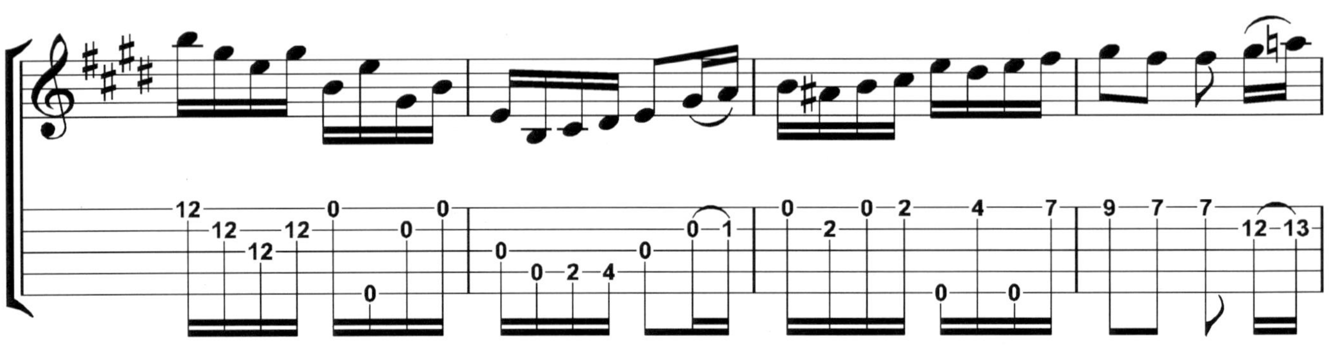

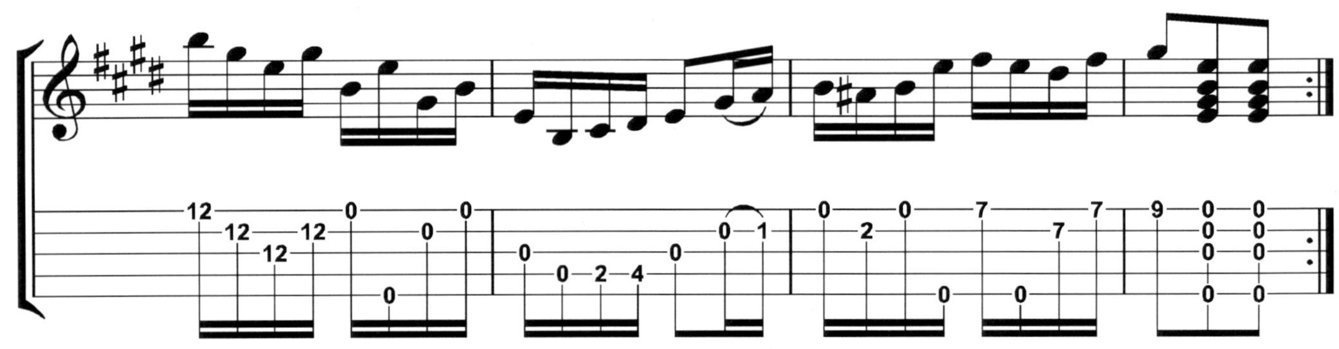

26. The Wind Up Irish Reel

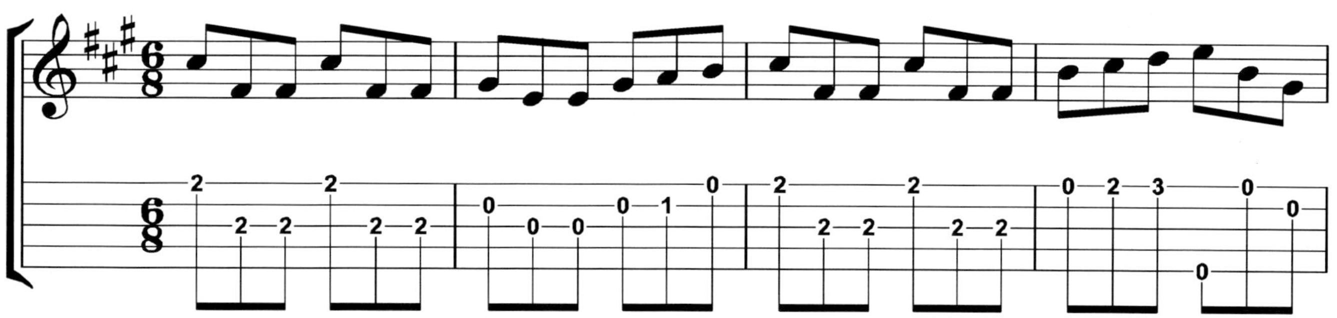

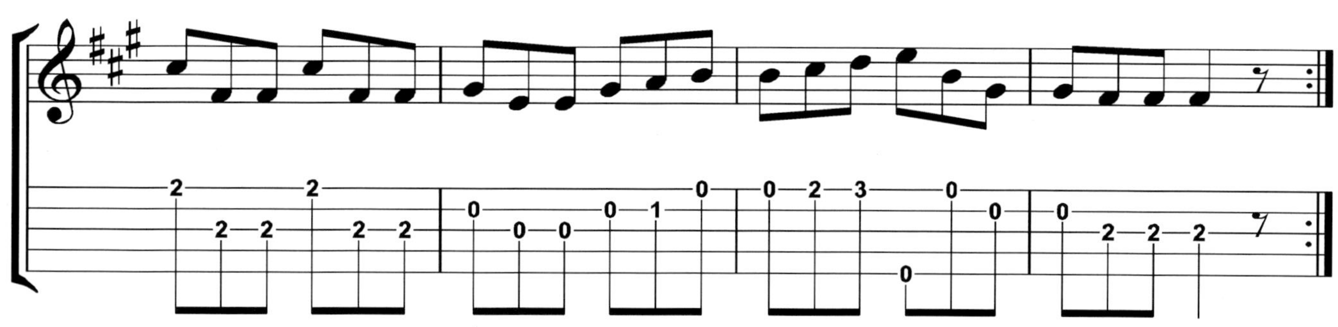

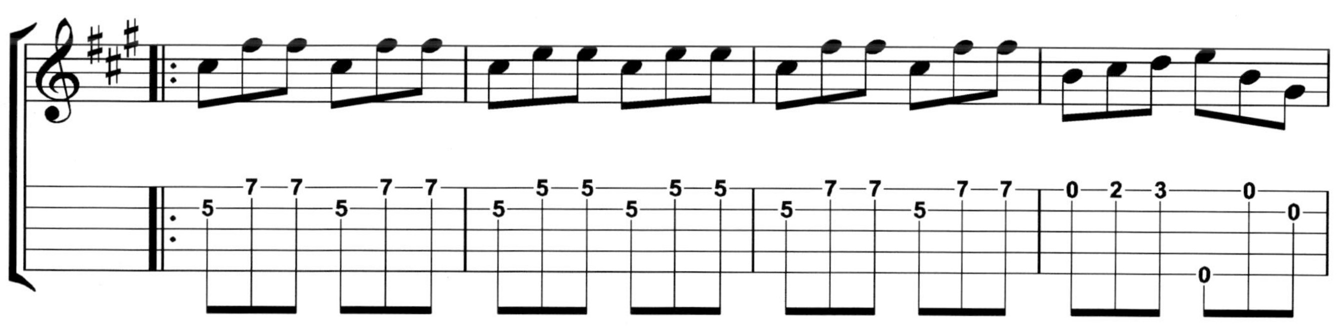

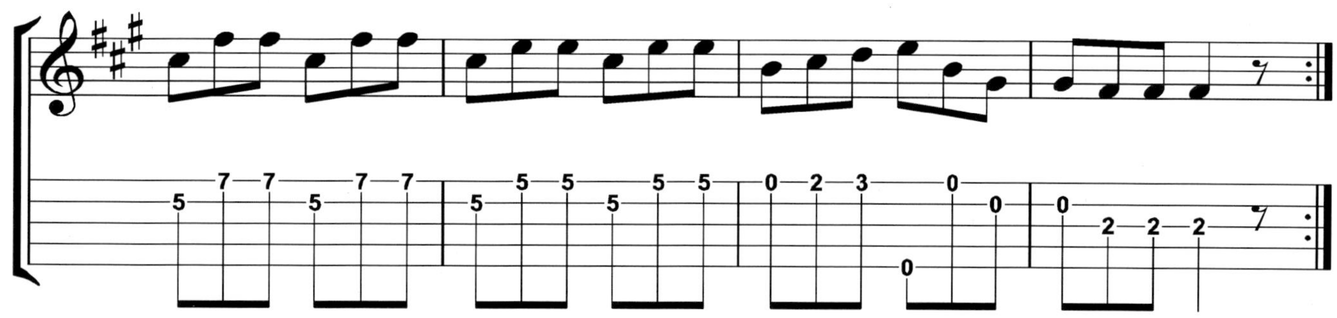

27. Johnny's Best Reel

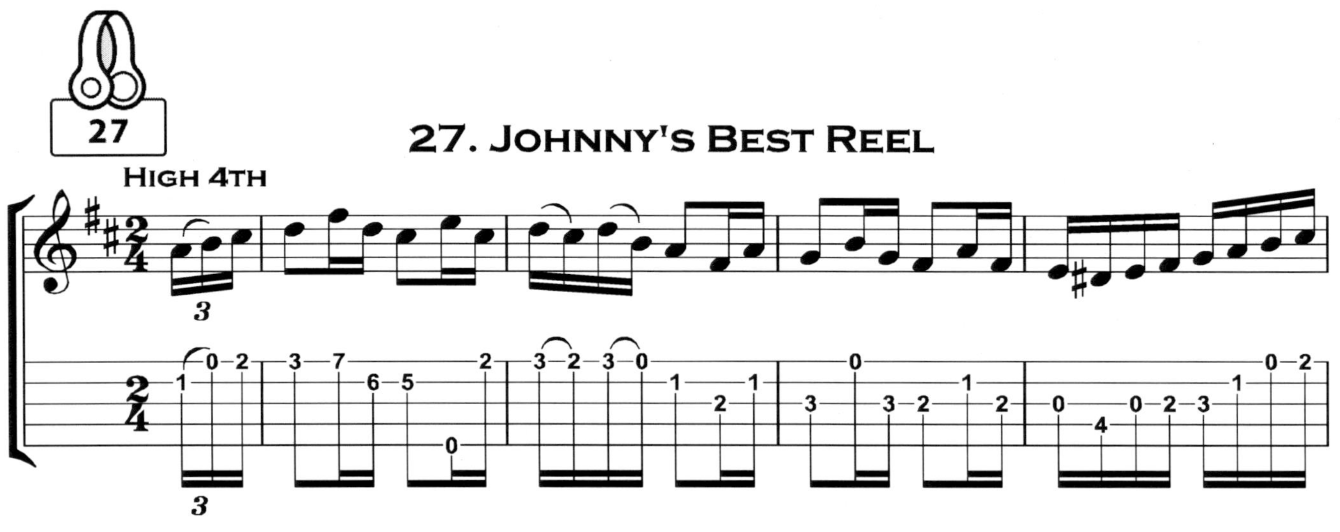

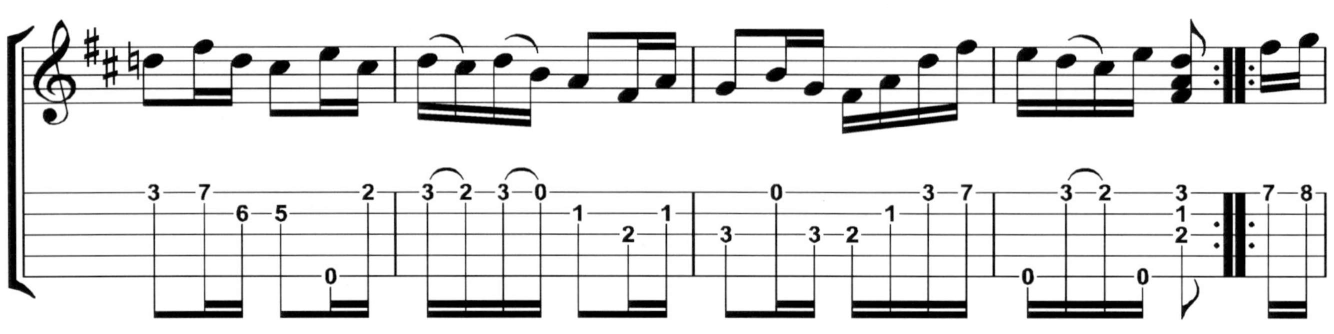

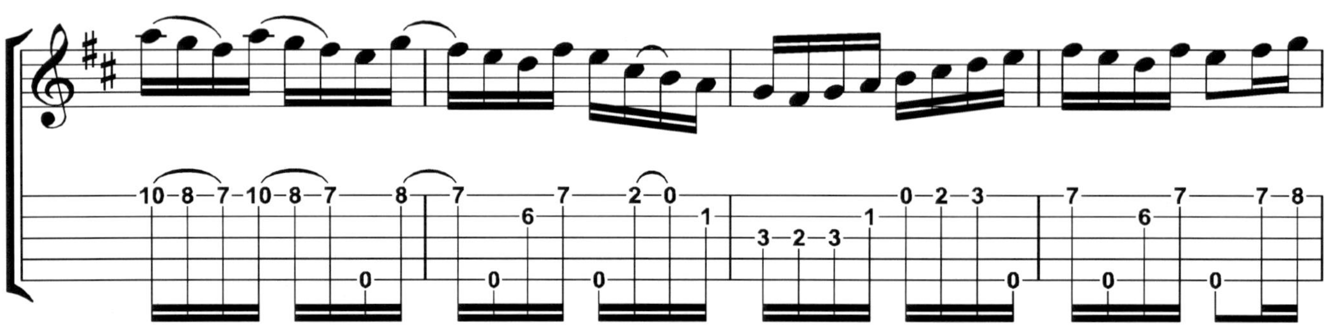

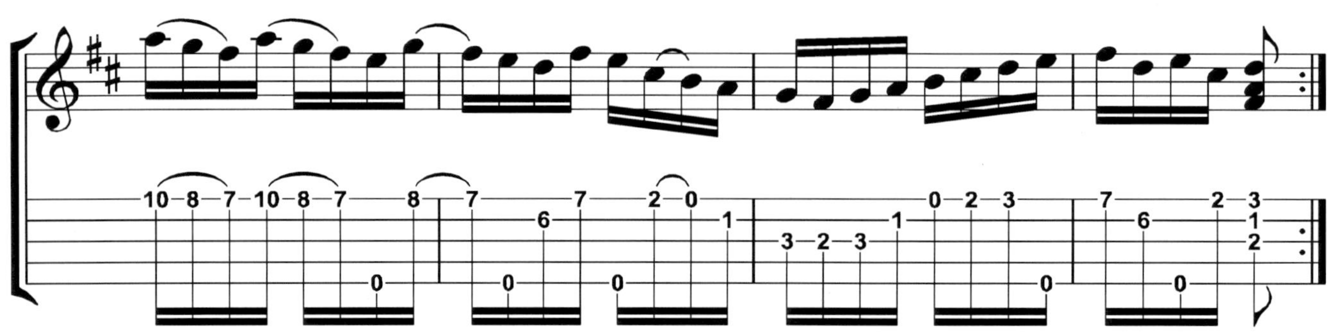

28. Jumping Jacks Reel

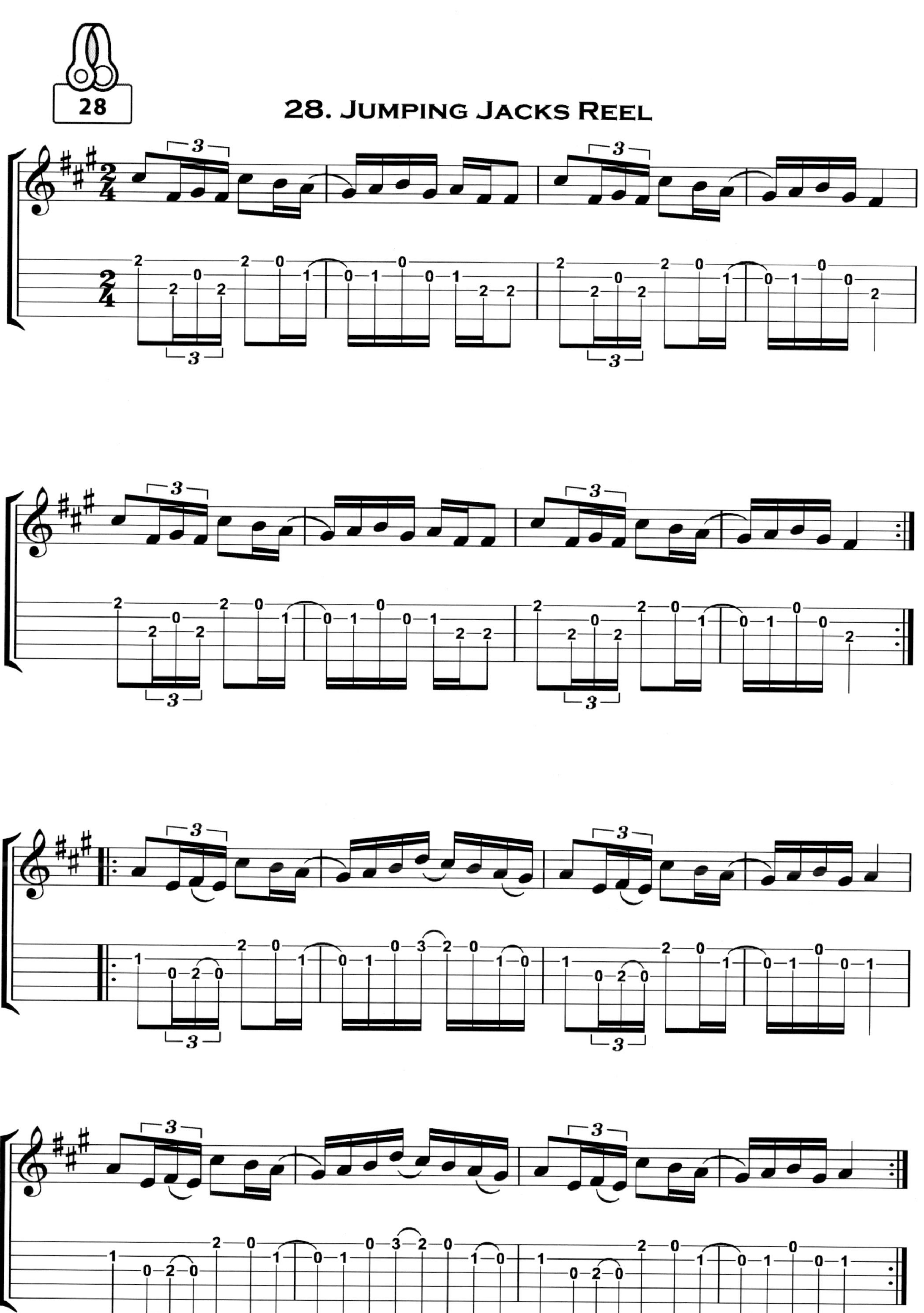

29. Neat and Graceful Clog

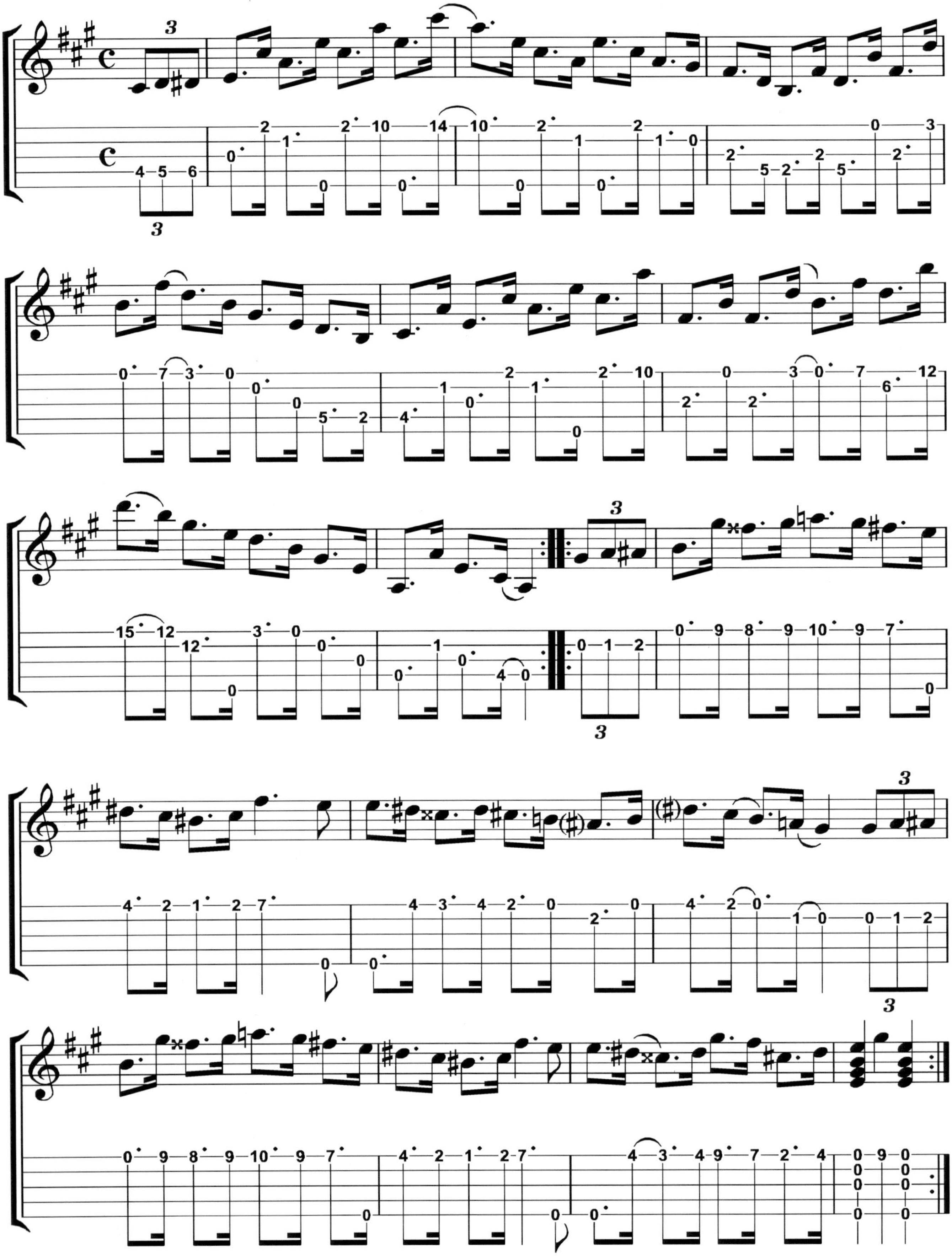

This page has been left blank to avoid an awkward page turn.

30. Twisted Rope Jig

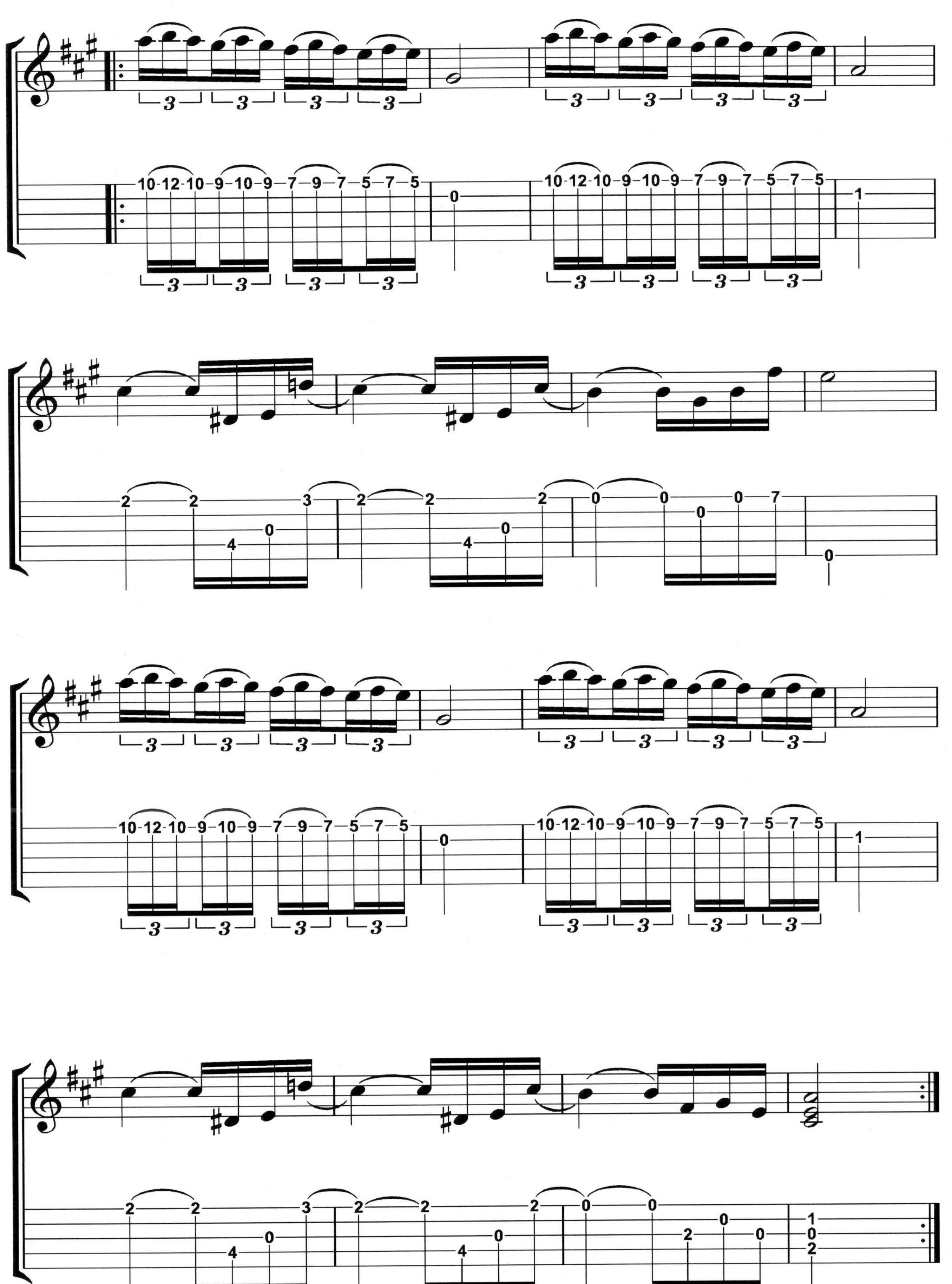

31

31. Wooden Shoes Clog Dance

32

32. Electric Light Reel

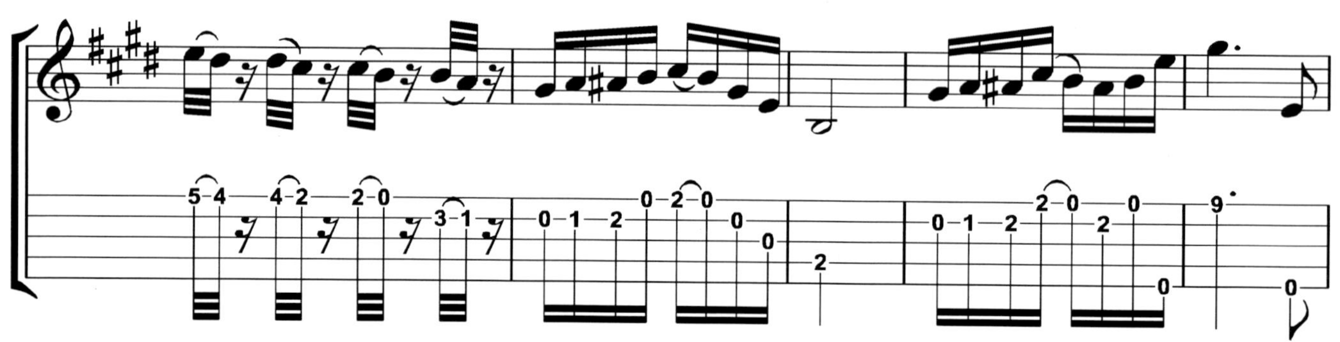

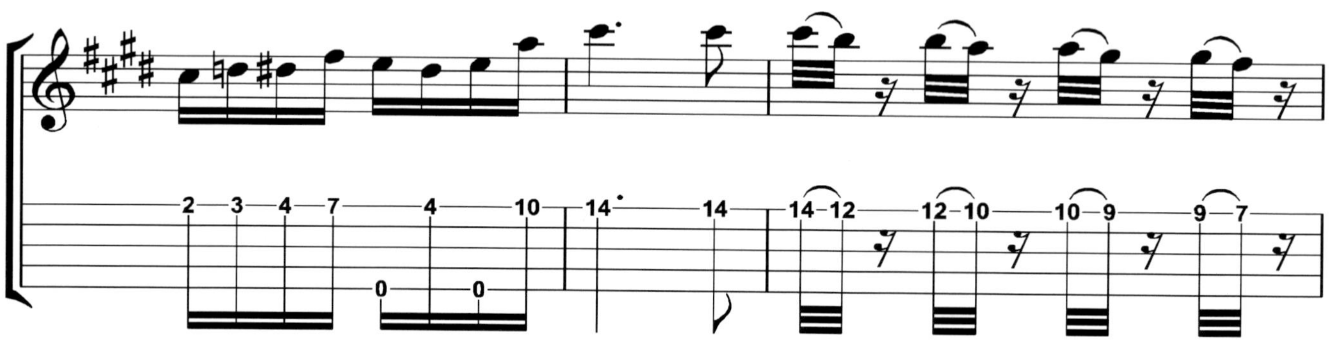

H = Harmonics

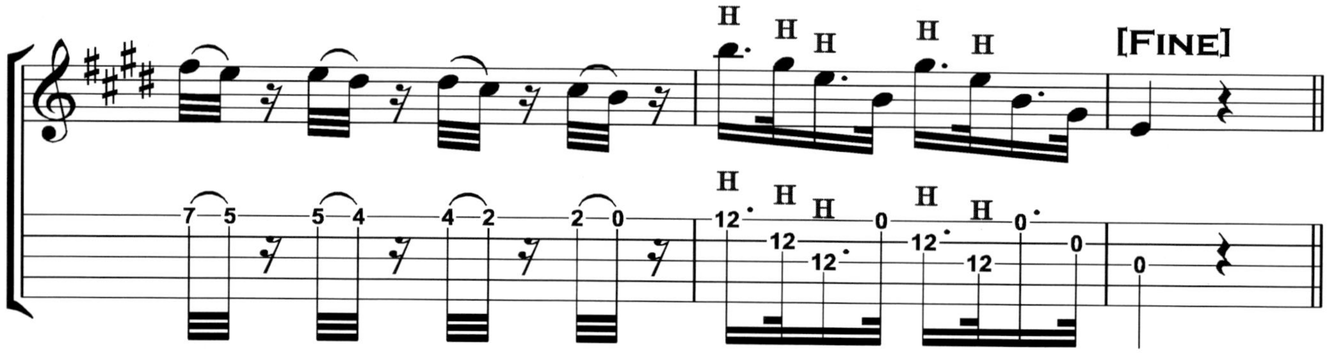

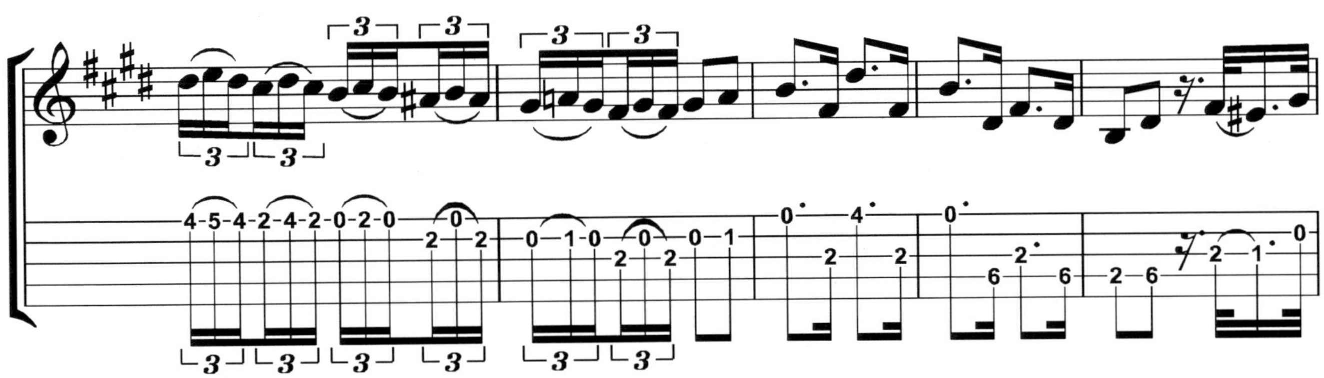

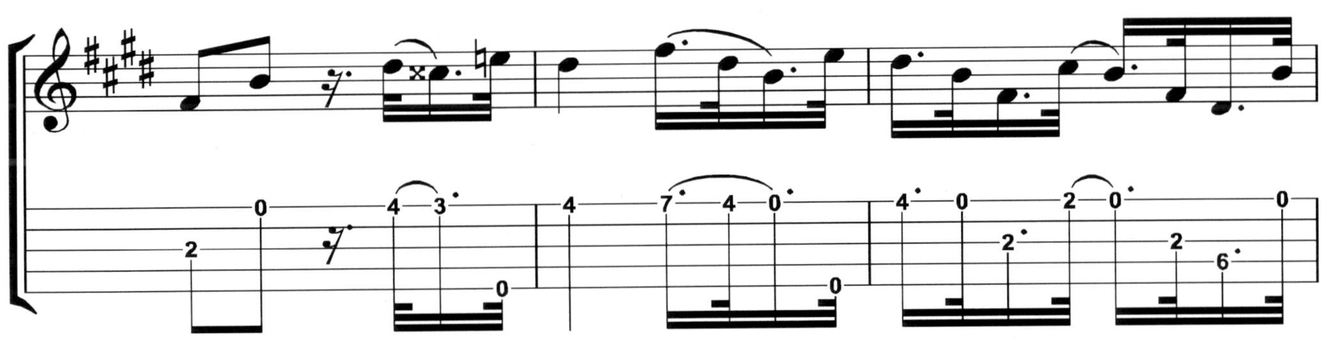

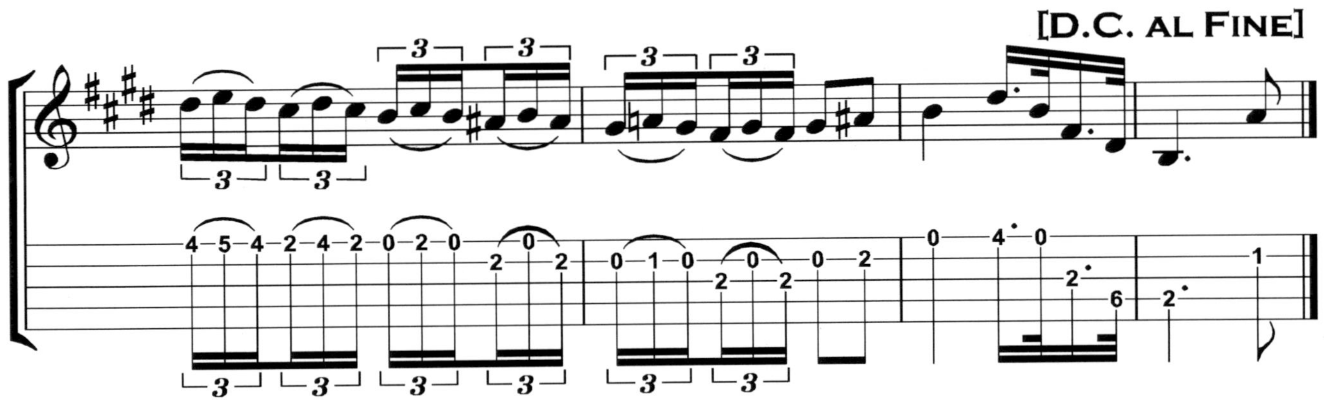
[D.C. AL FINE]

33. I'm Happy Clog Dance

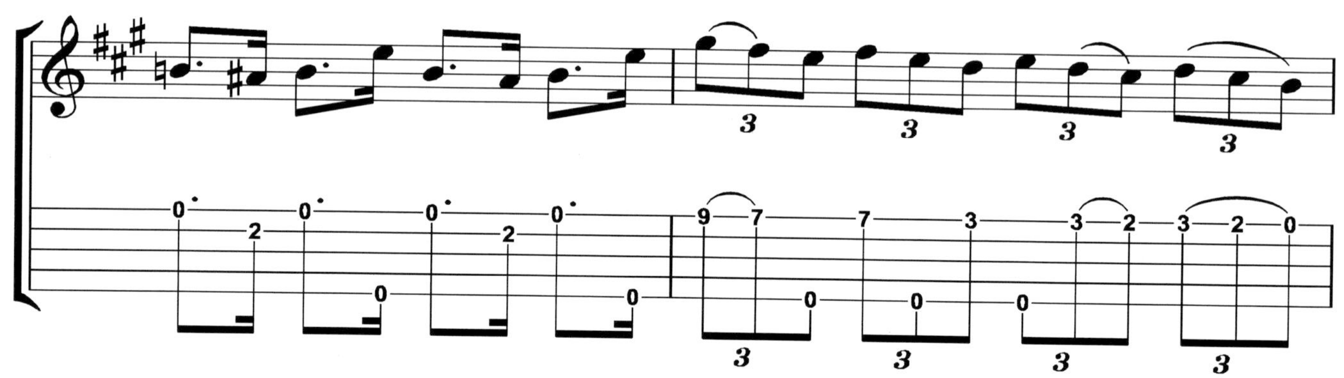

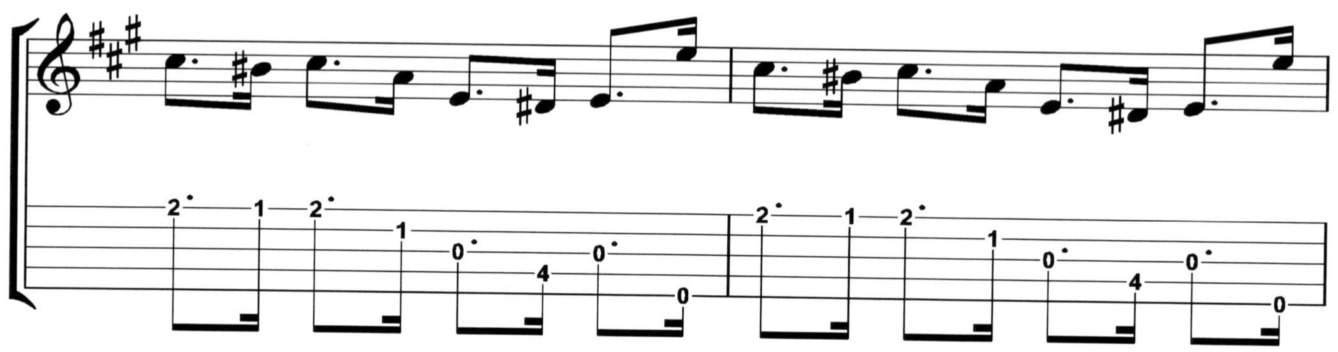

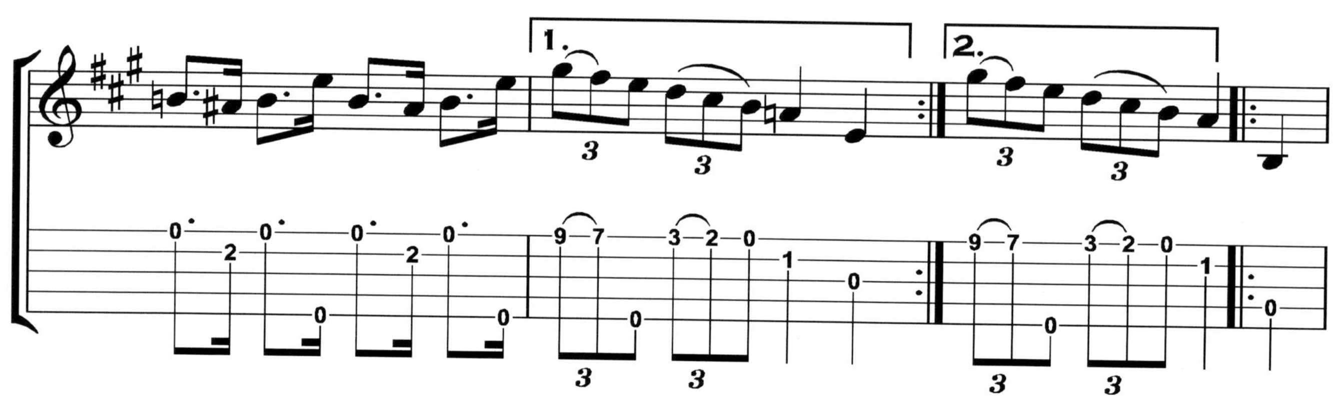

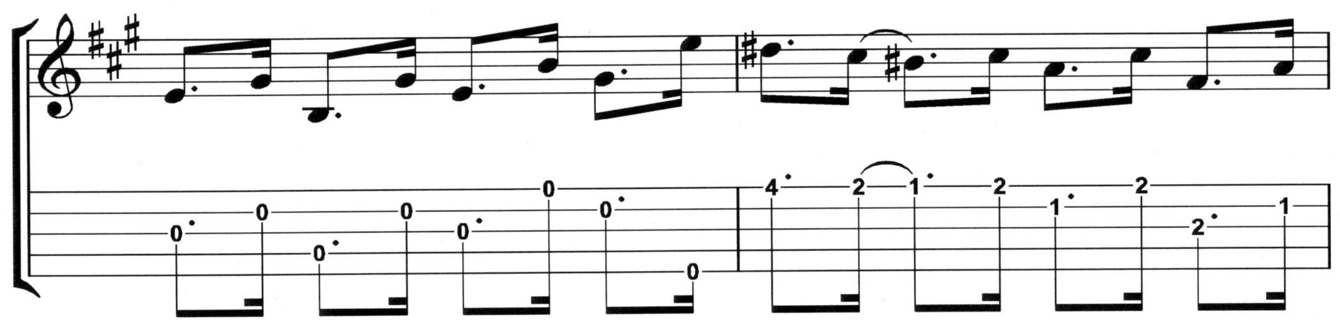

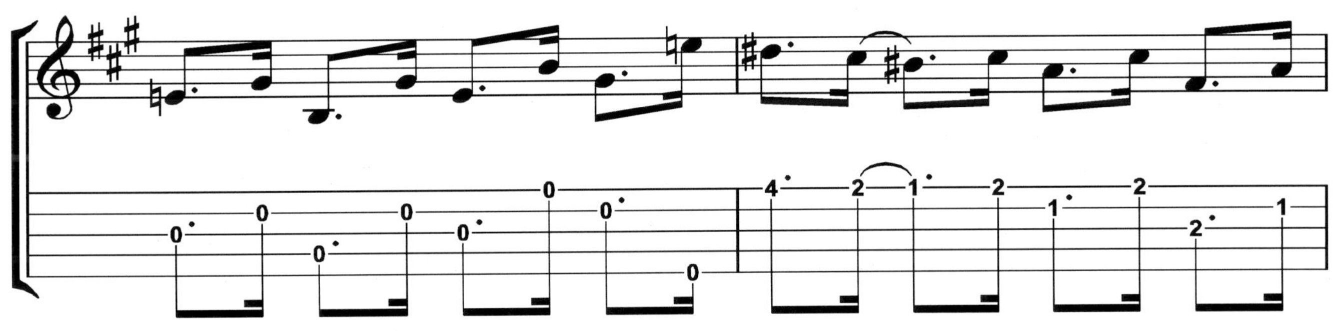

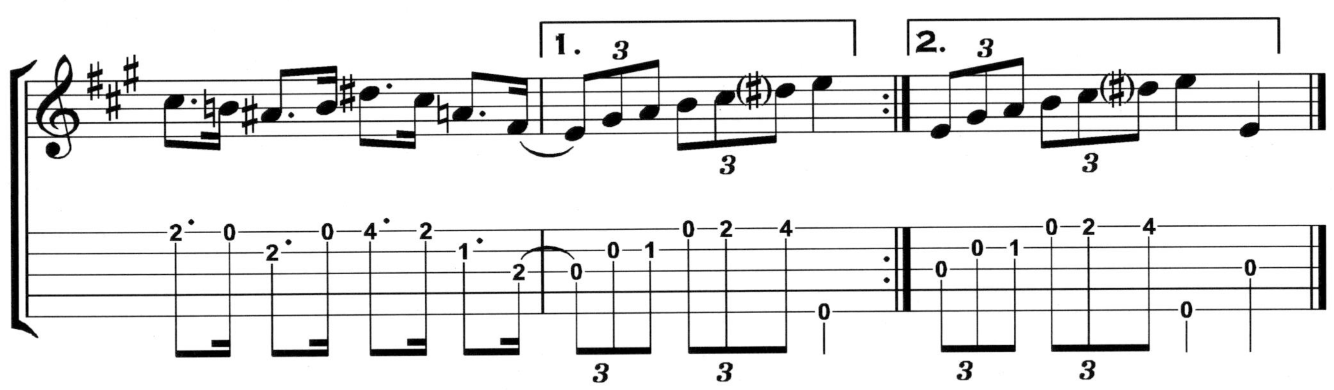
1.
2.

34. On the Barn Floor Jig

High 4th
Andante

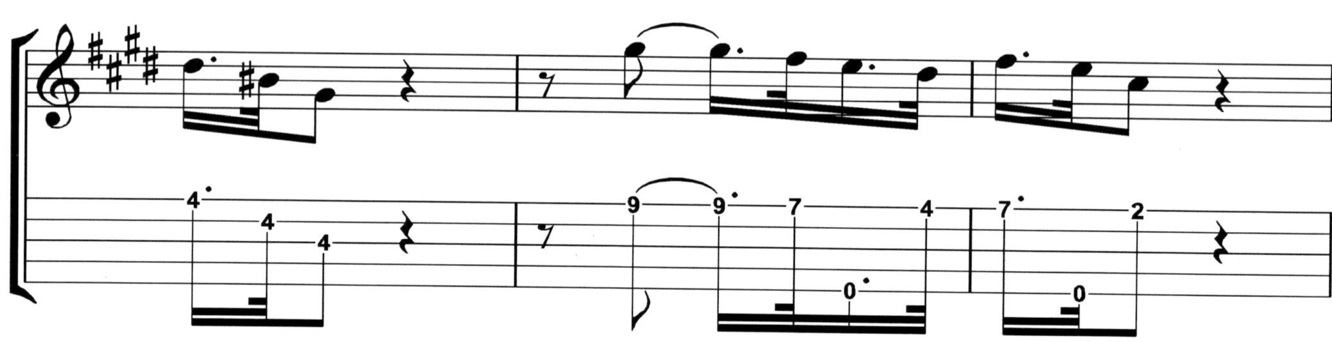

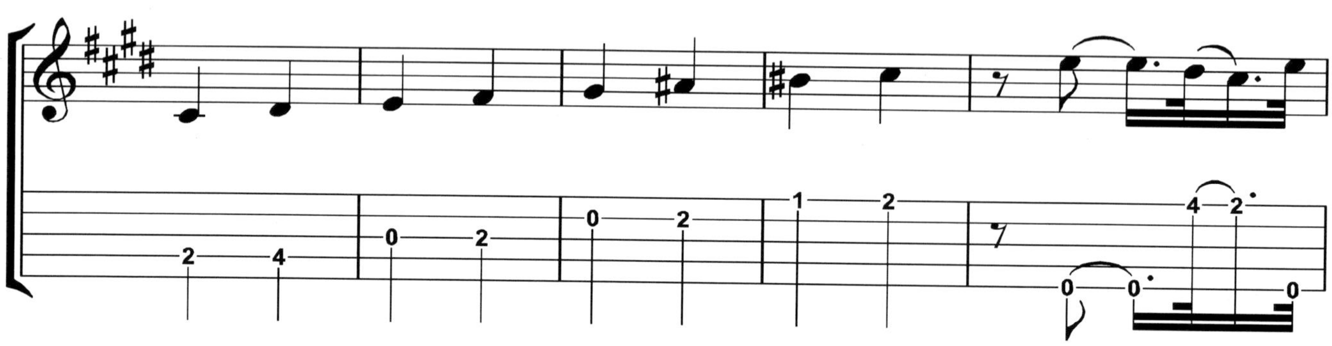

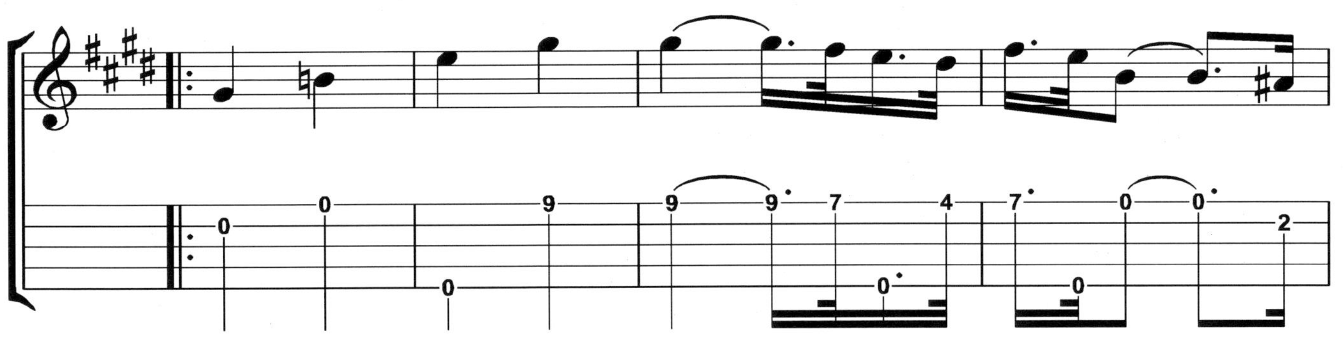

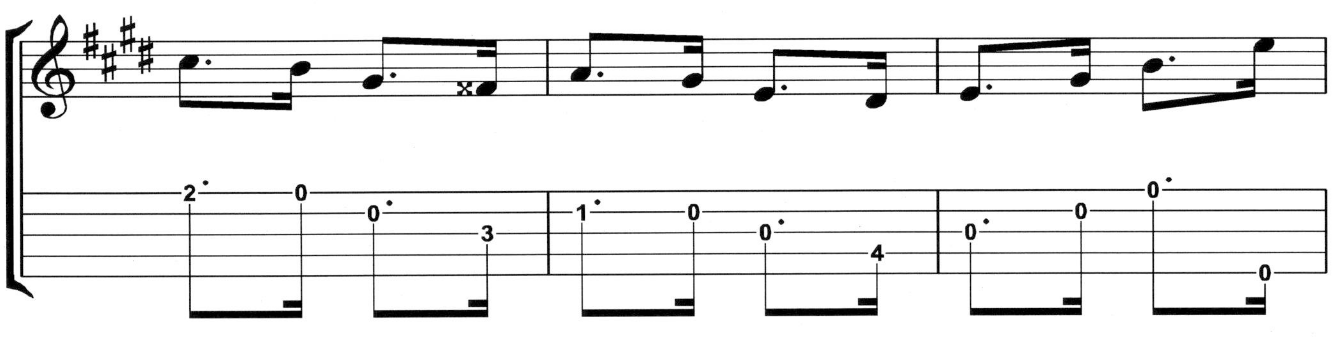

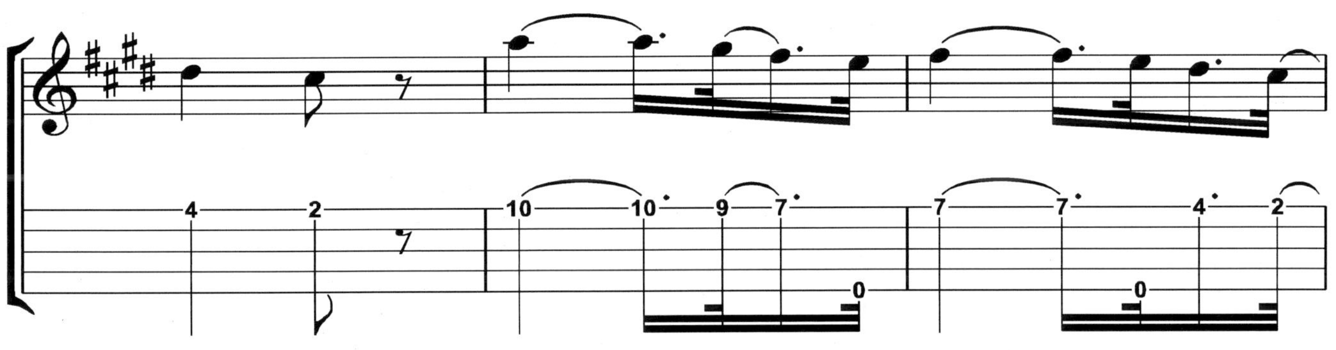

S = Slide
S
S
S
S

35. "Too Utterly Too" Clog Dance

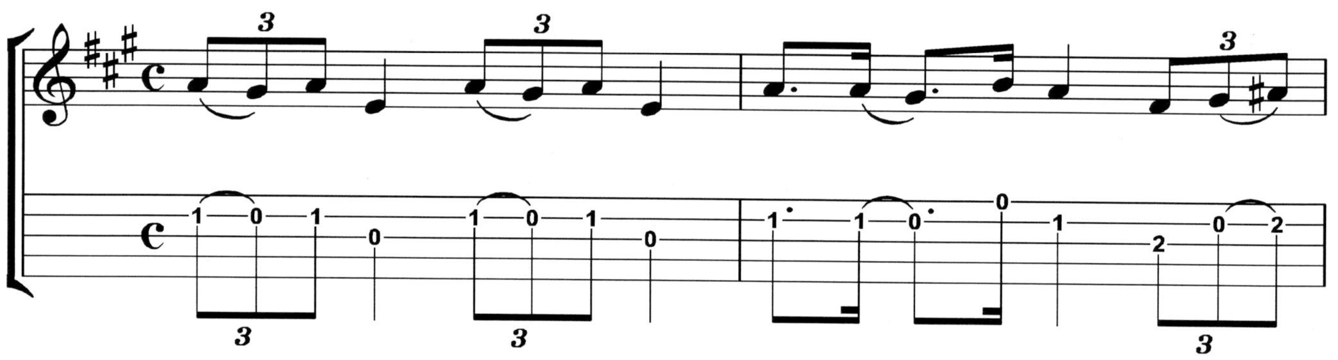

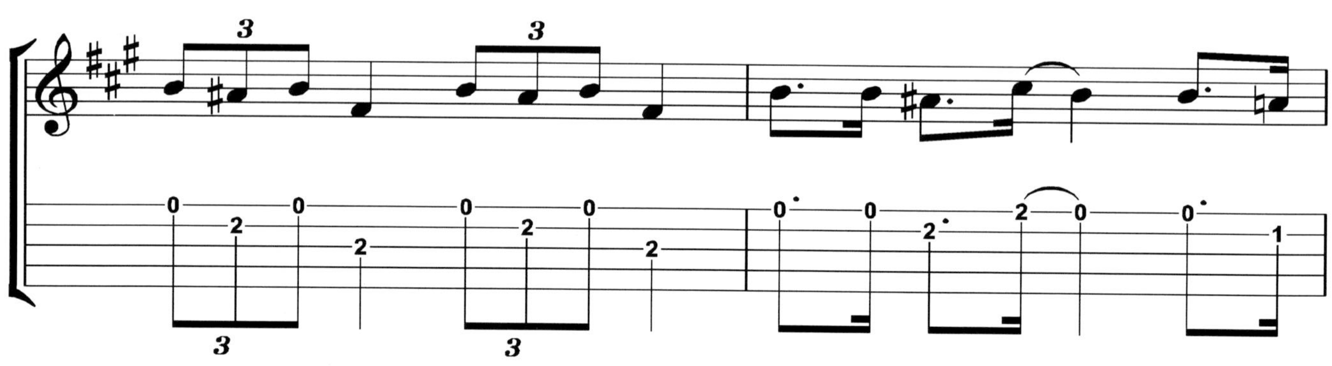

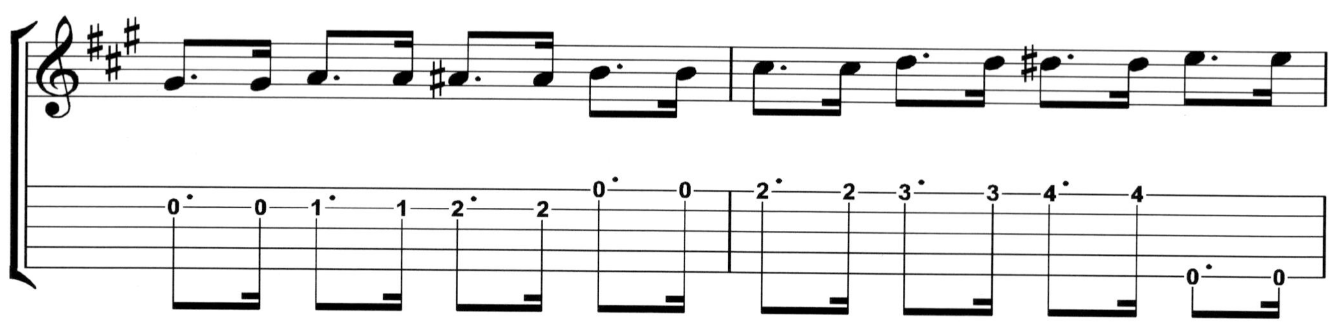

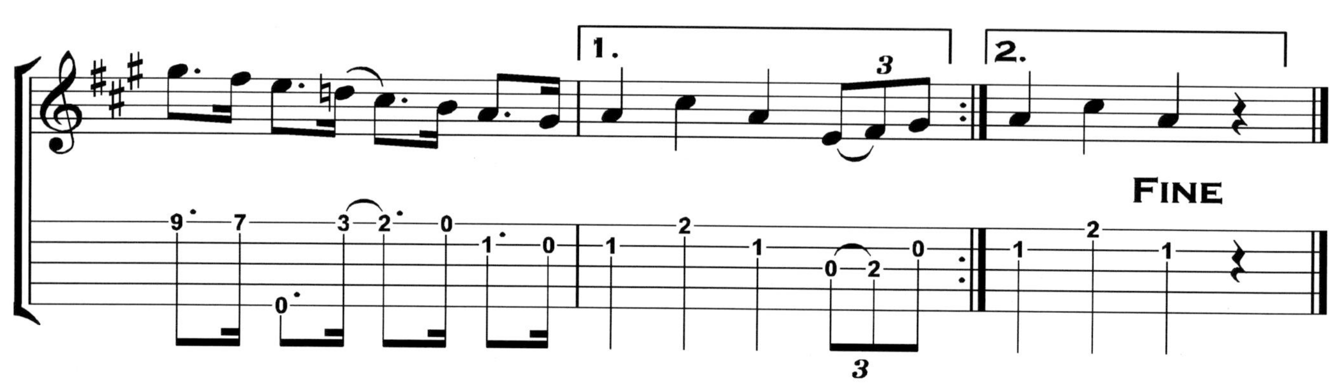

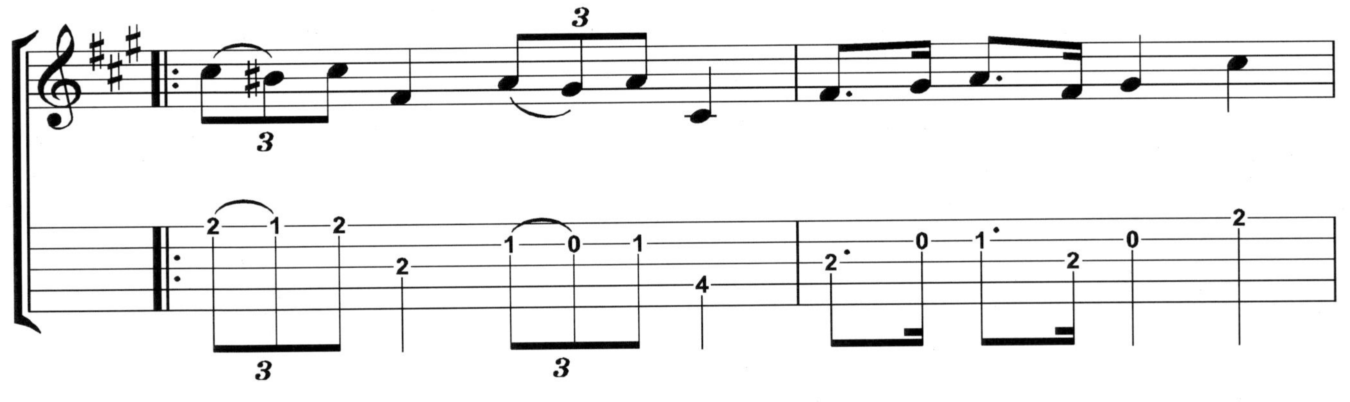

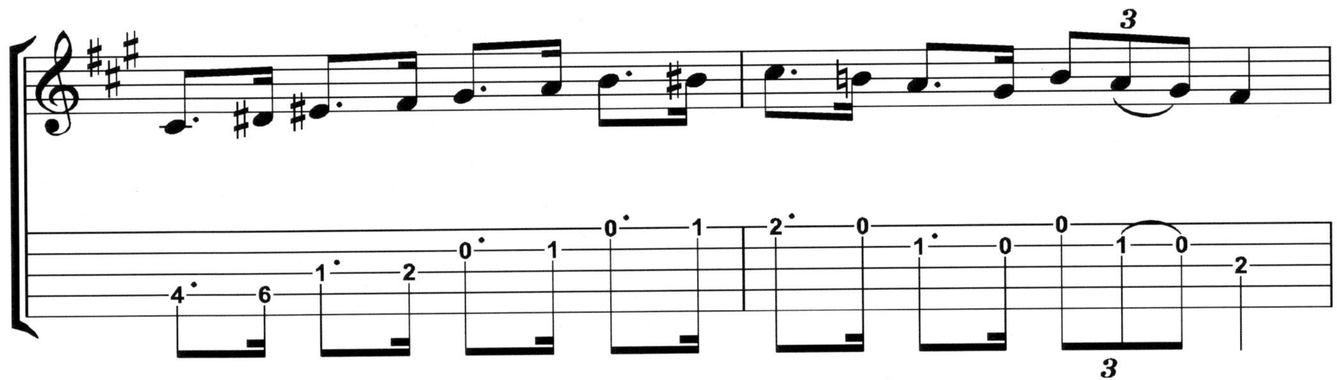

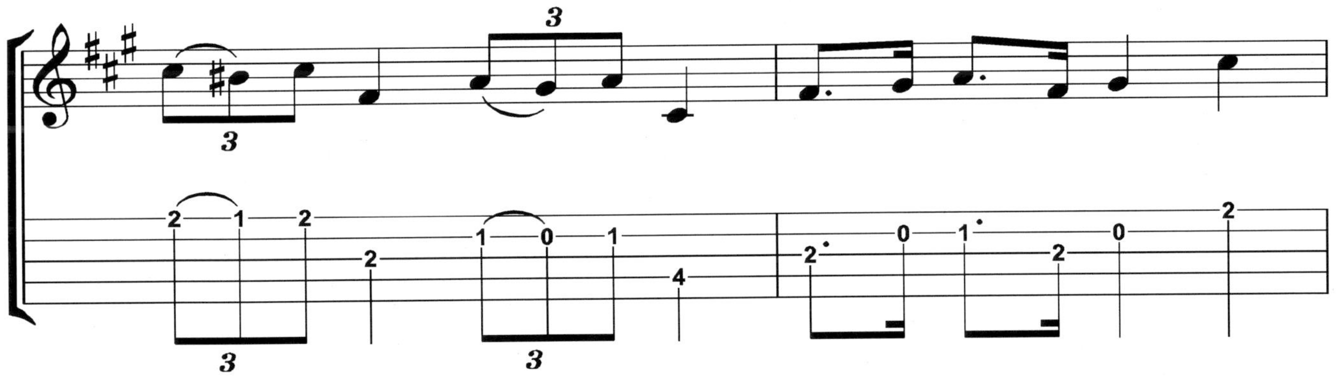

D.C. al Fine

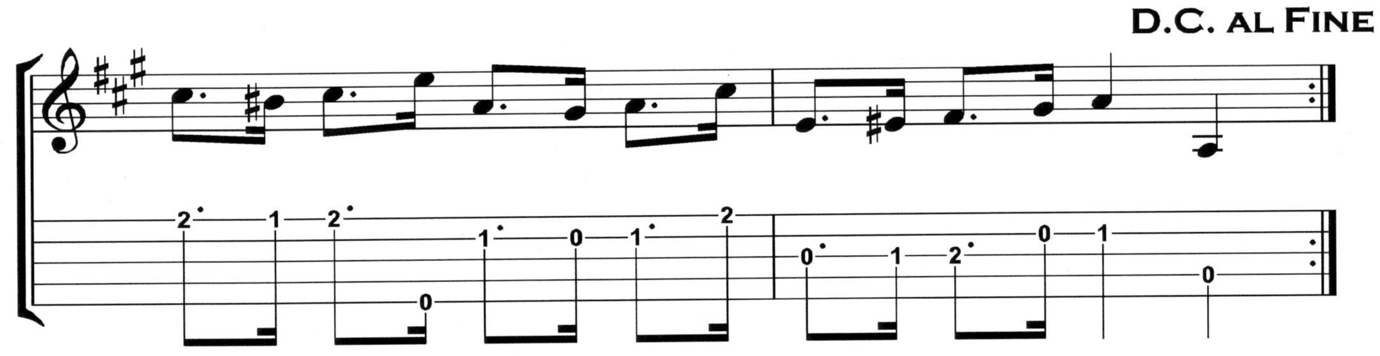

36. Go As You Please Walk Around

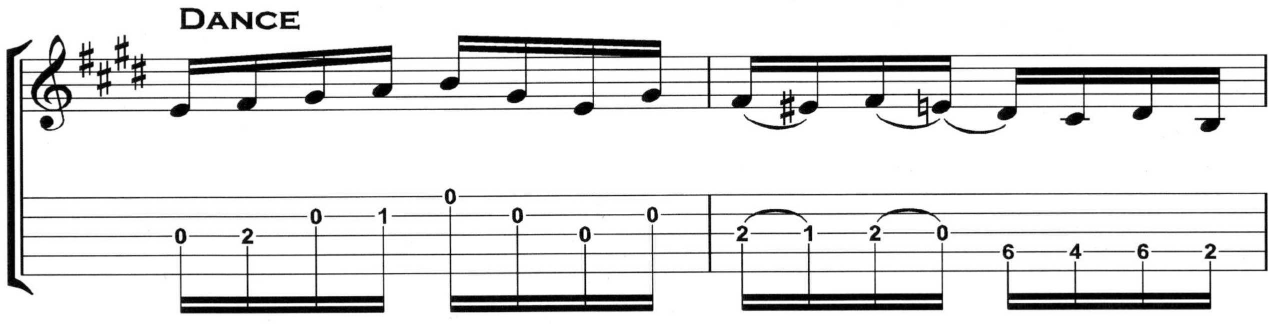
Dance

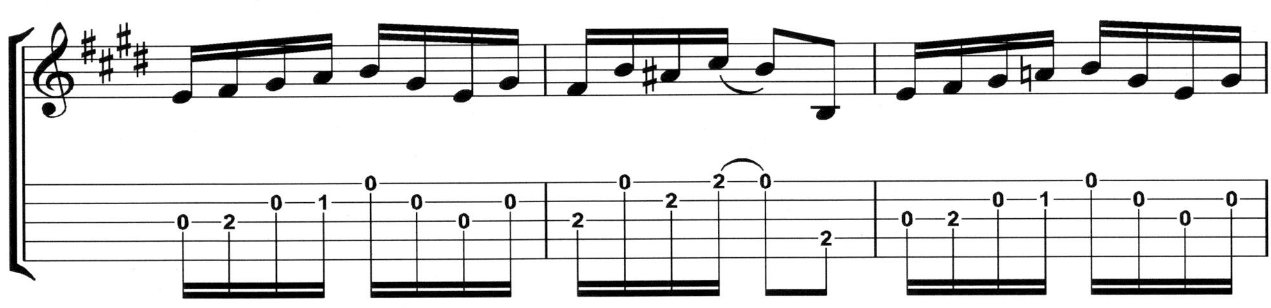

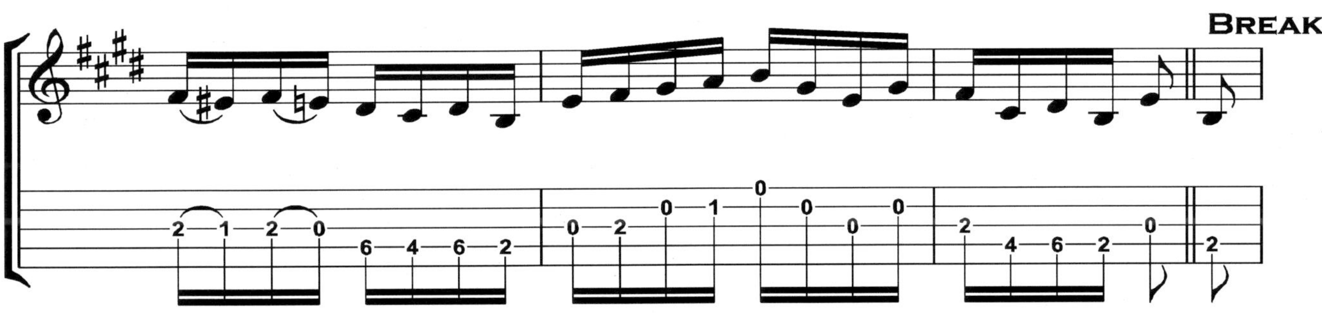
Break

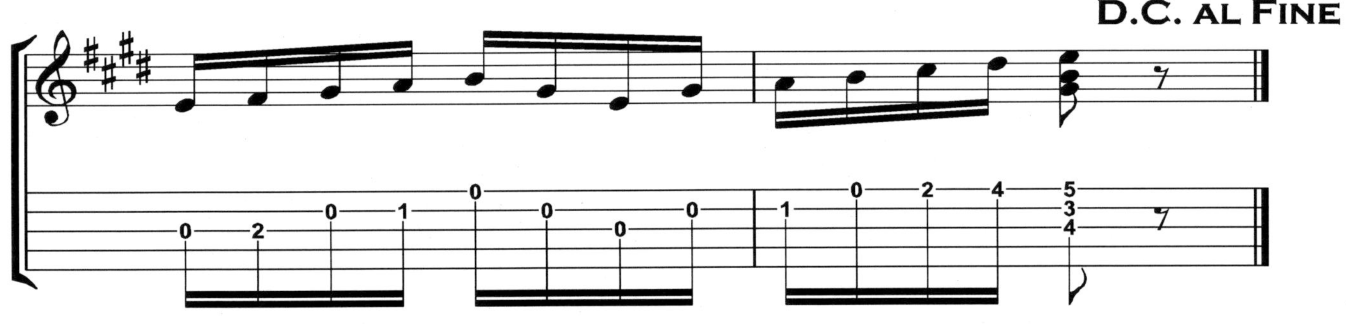
D.C. al Fine

37. Silver Spangles Clog Dance

High 4th

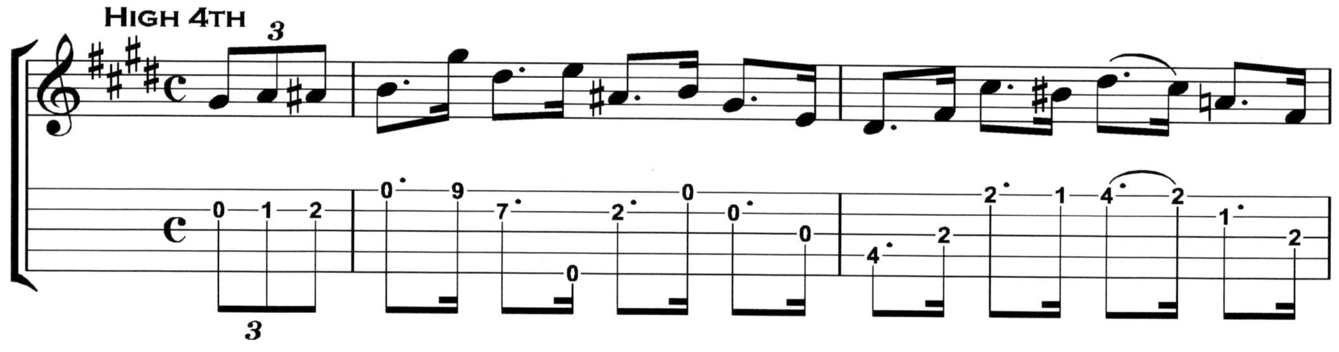

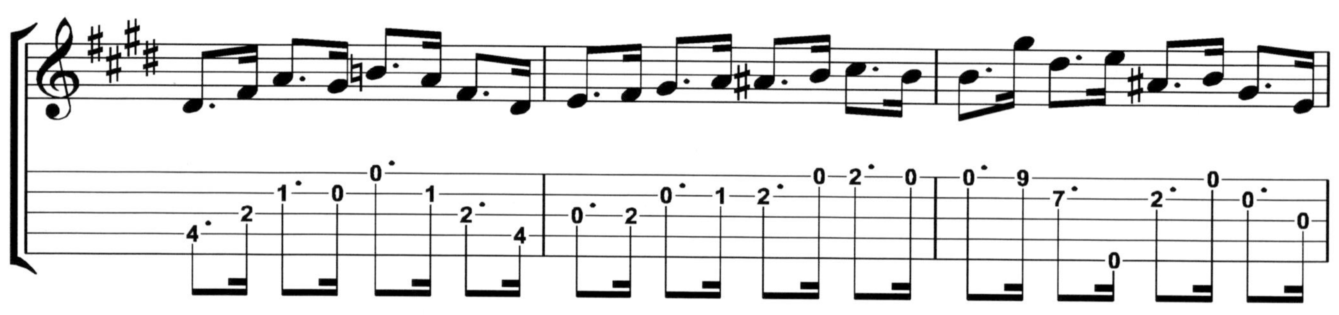

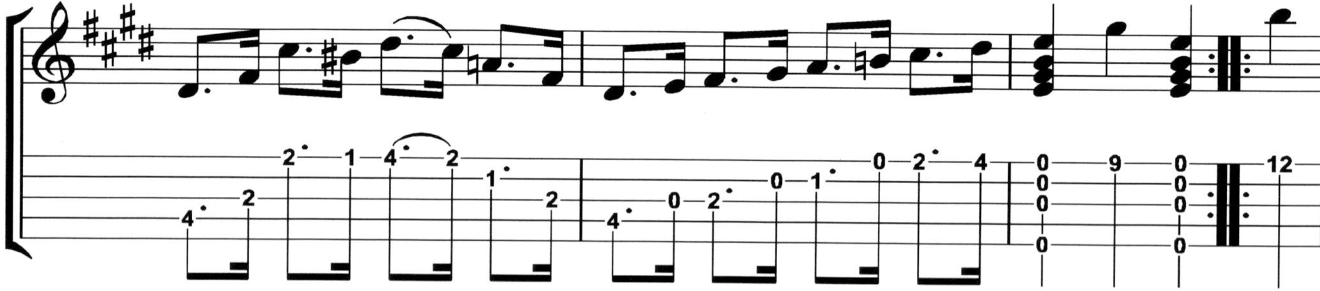

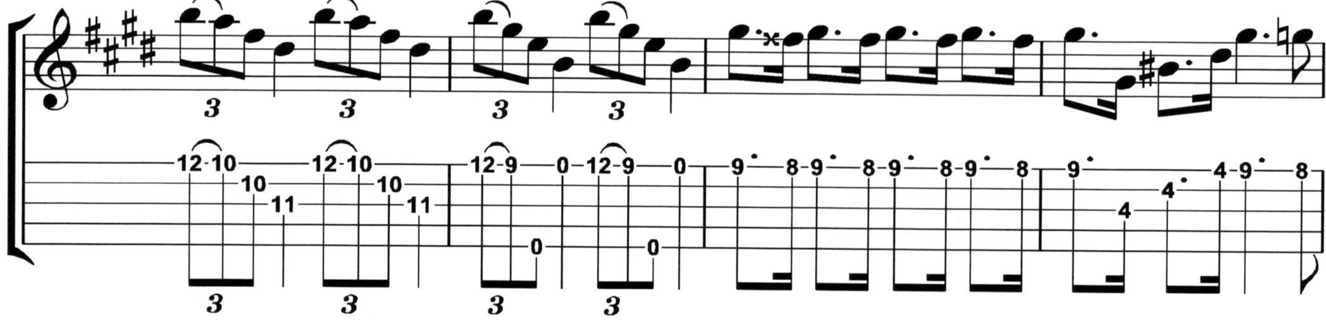

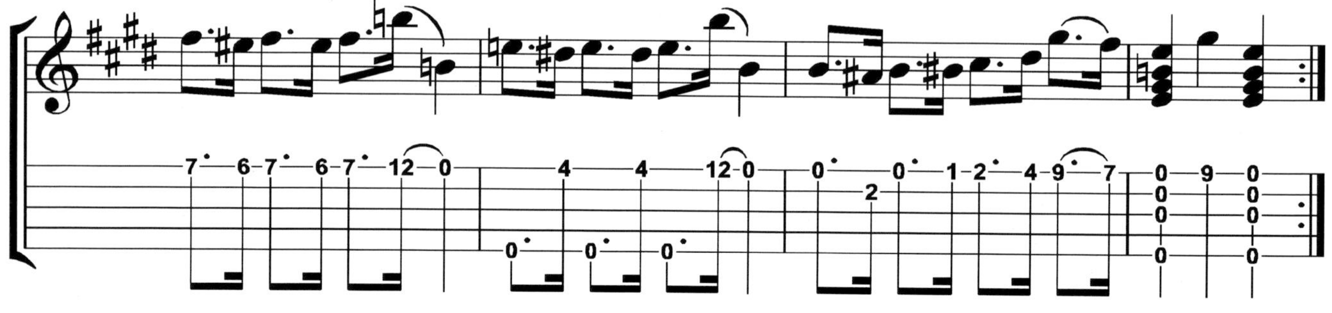

This page has been left blank to avoid an awkward page turn.

38. Sand Dance Jig

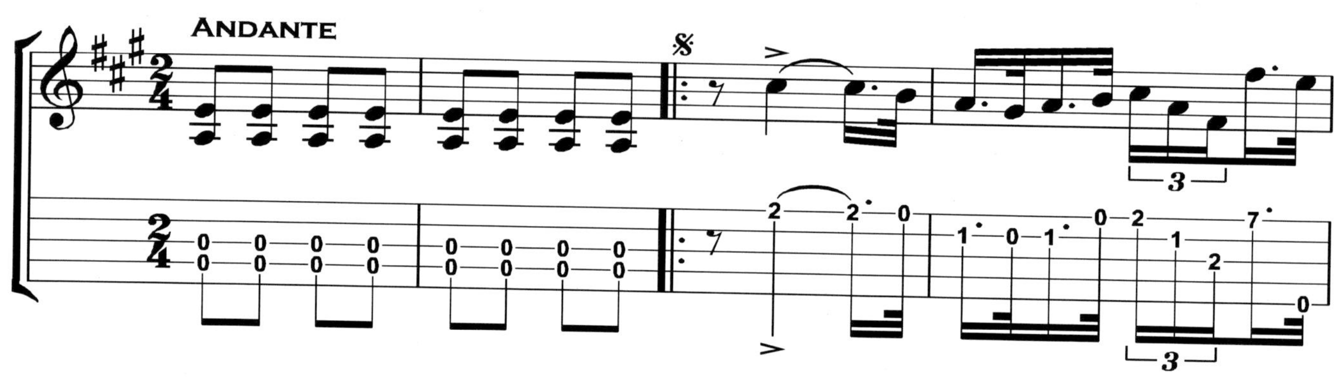

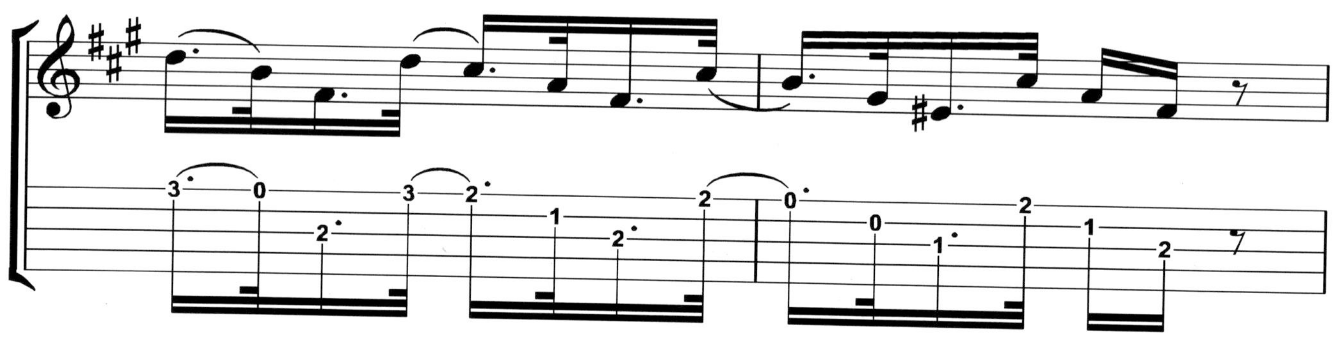

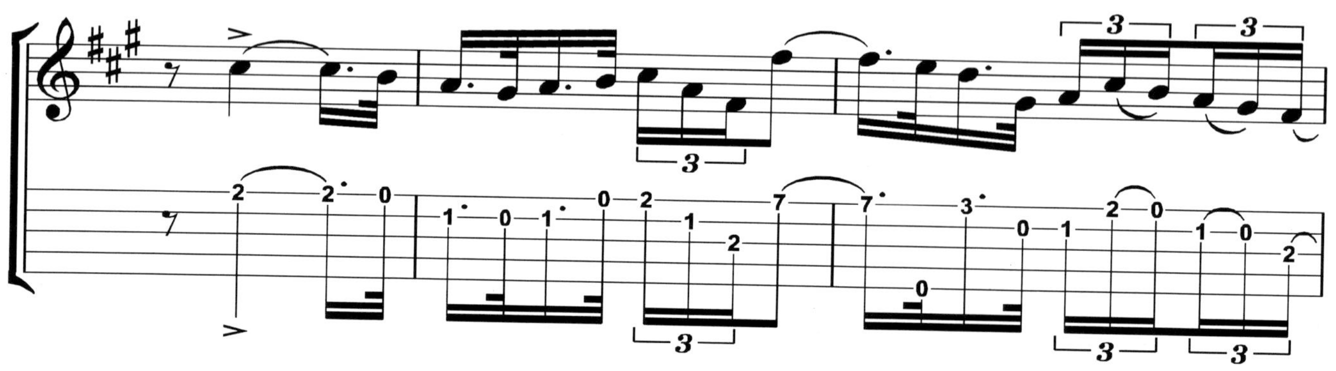

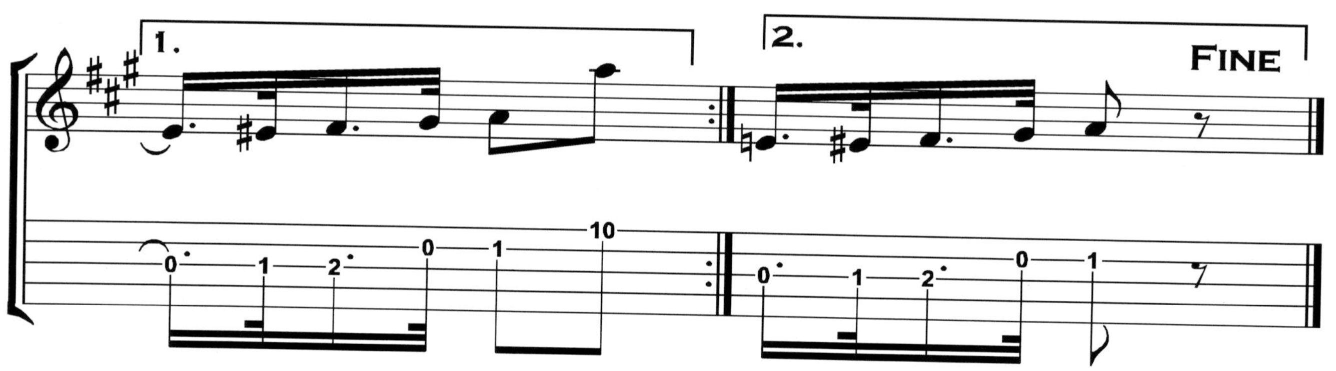

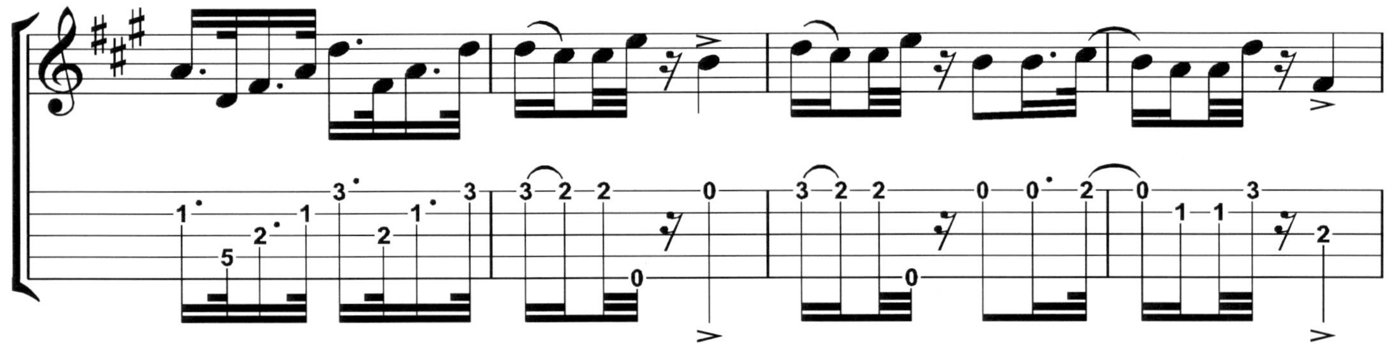

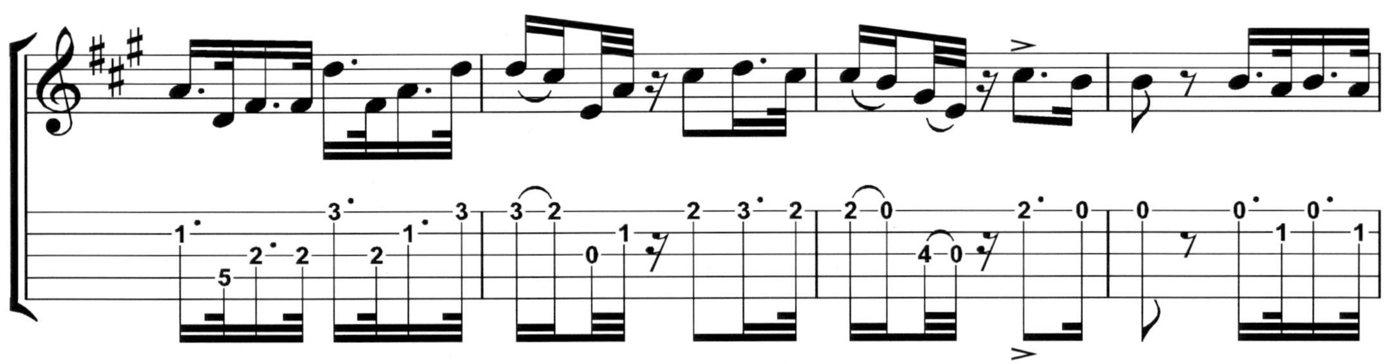

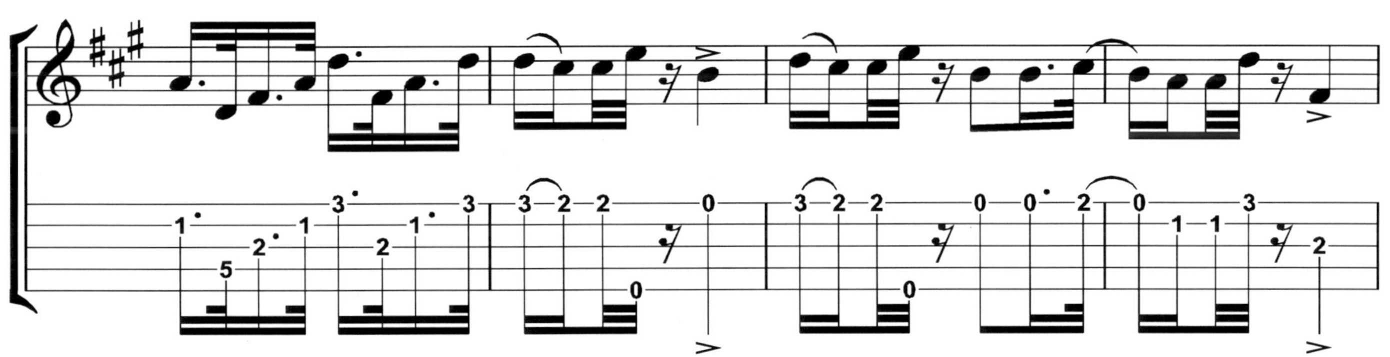

D.S. al Fine

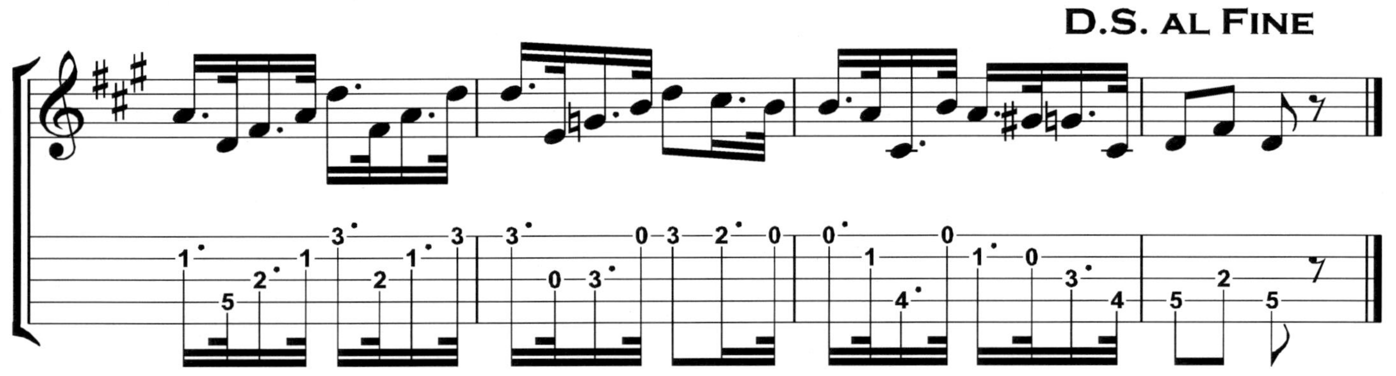

39. Aesthetic Clog Dance

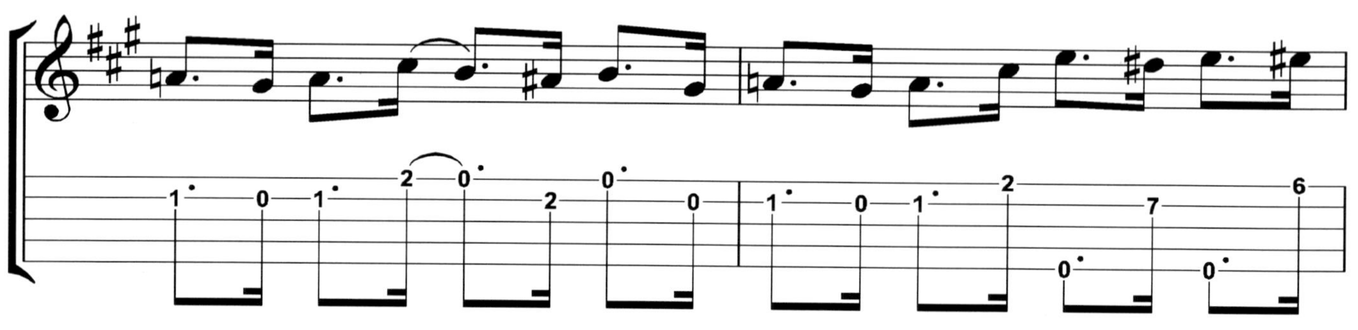

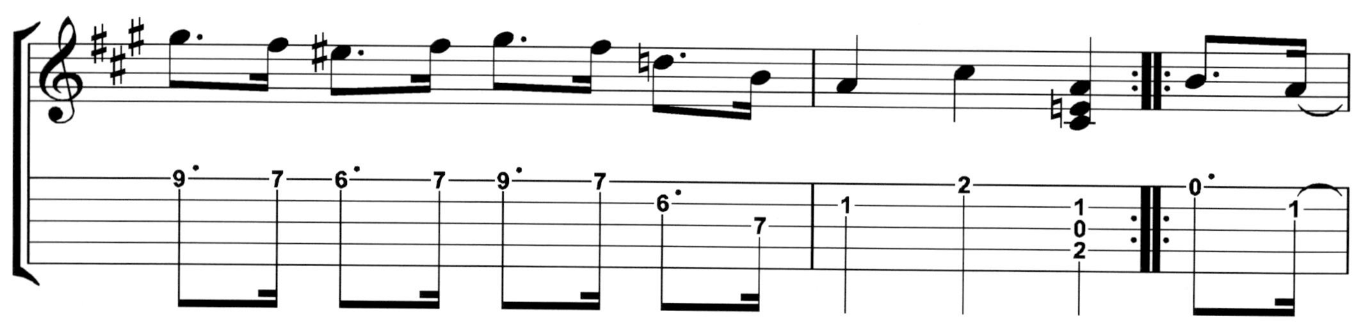

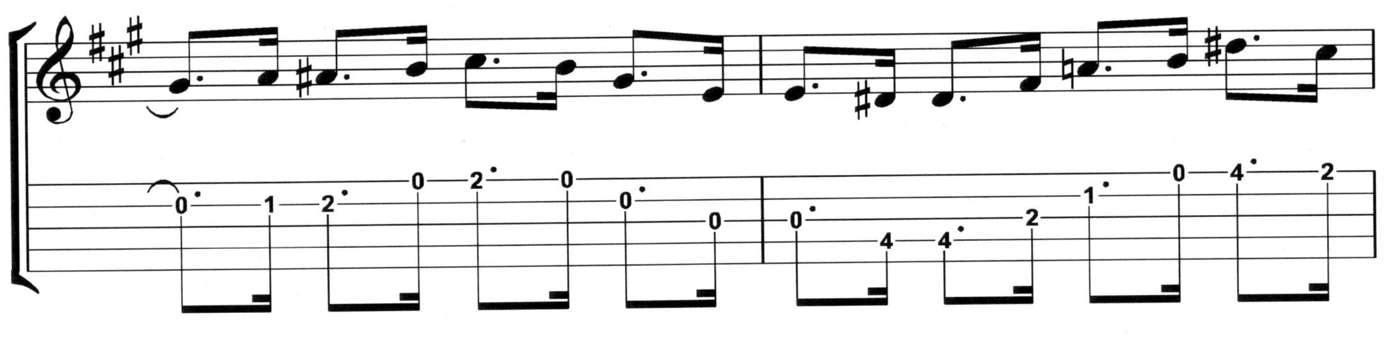

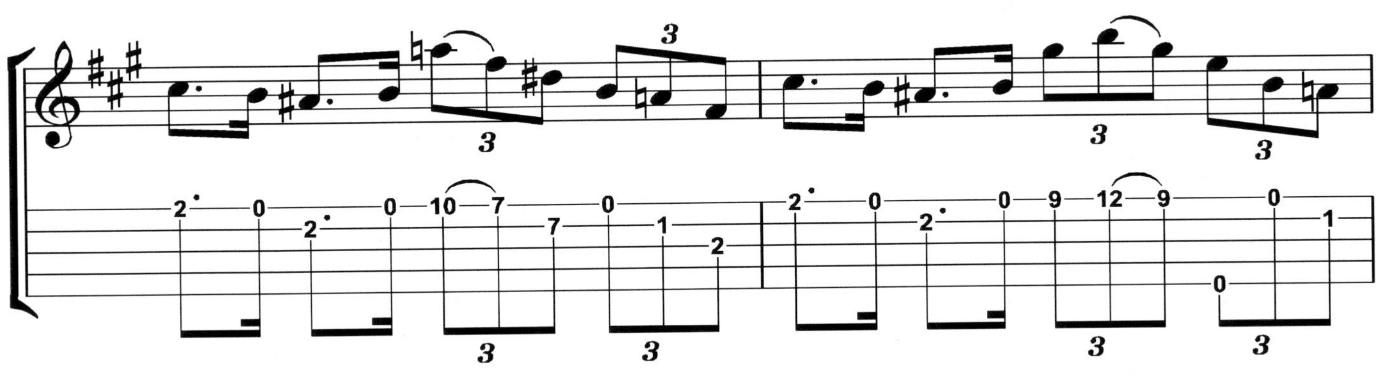

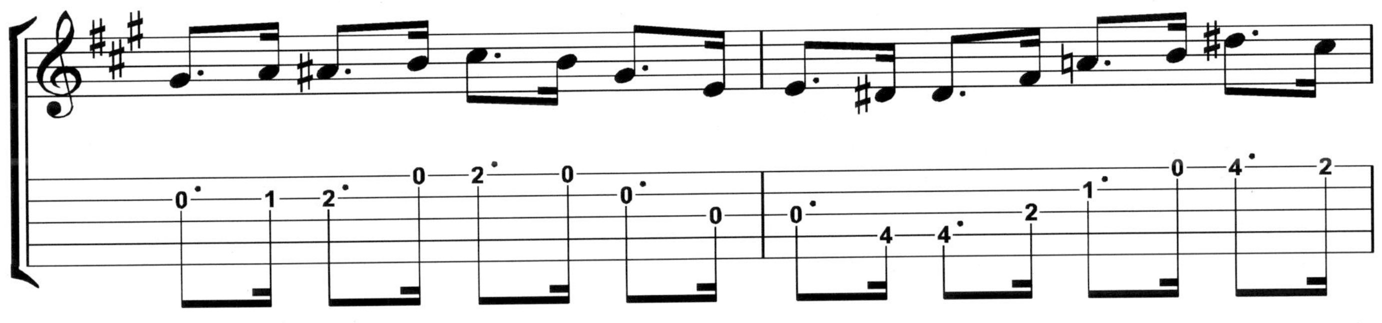

40. Heel Taps Jig

41 Big Four Walk Around

Dance

Dance

Break

Break

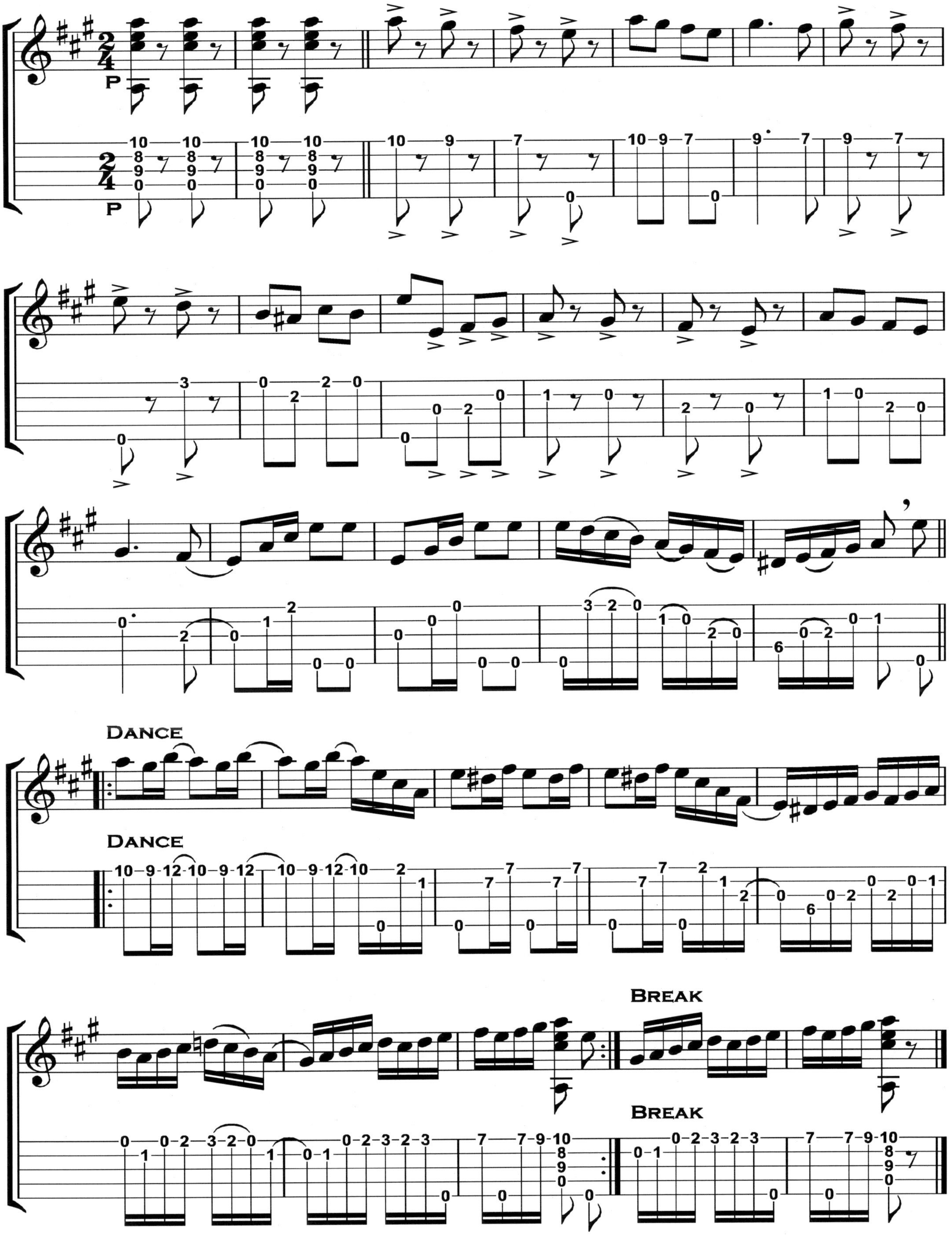

42. Mastodon Clog Dance

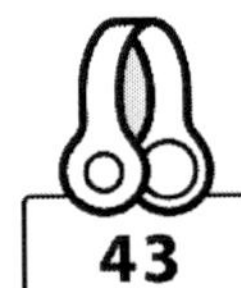

43. Aunt Pricella's Party Walk Around

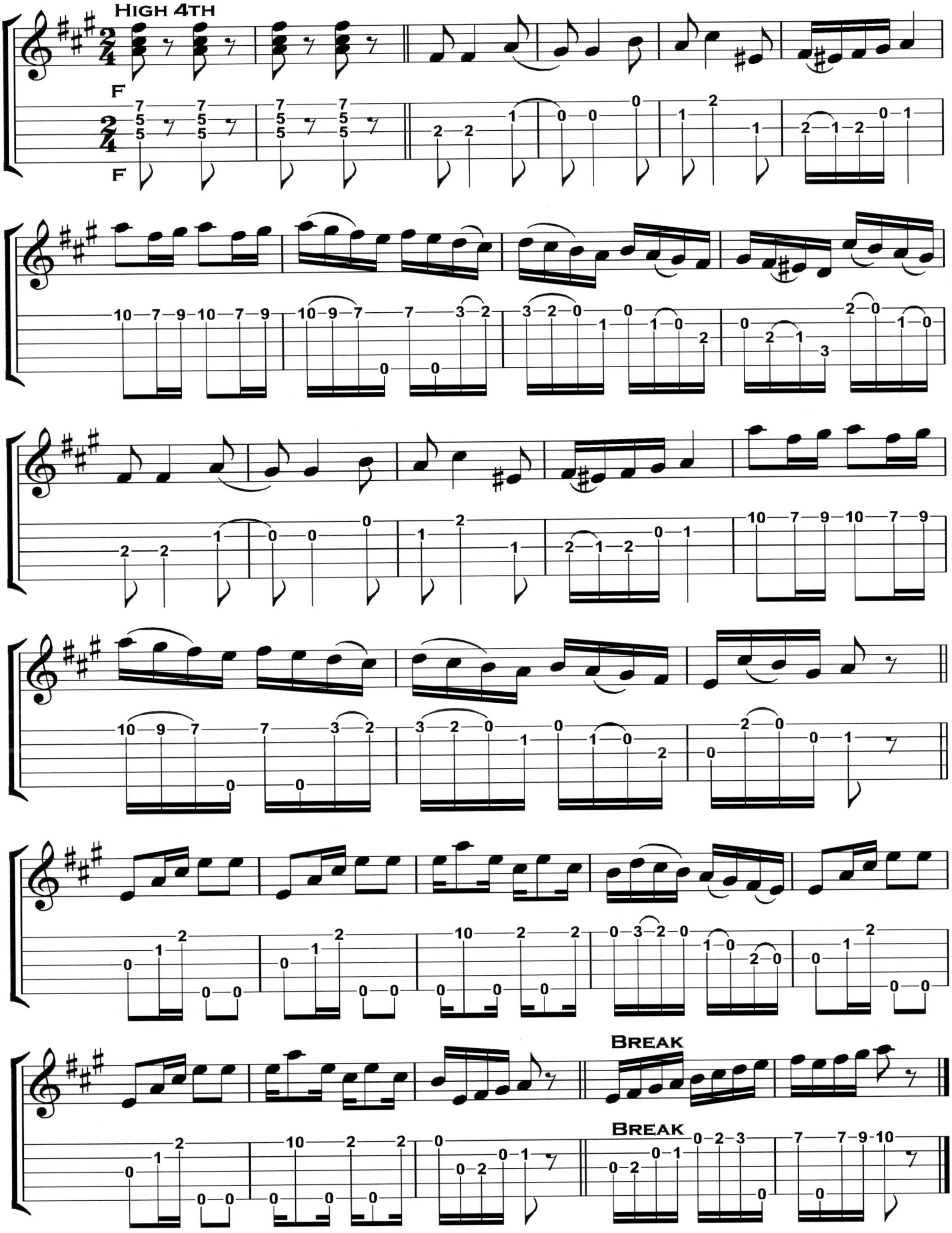

High 4th

F

F

Break

Break

44. Artistic Jig

45. Light and Airy Clog Dance

High 4th

46
46. On the Quiet Jig
Fine
D.S. al Fine

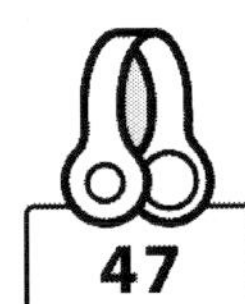

47. Takes the Cake Walk Around

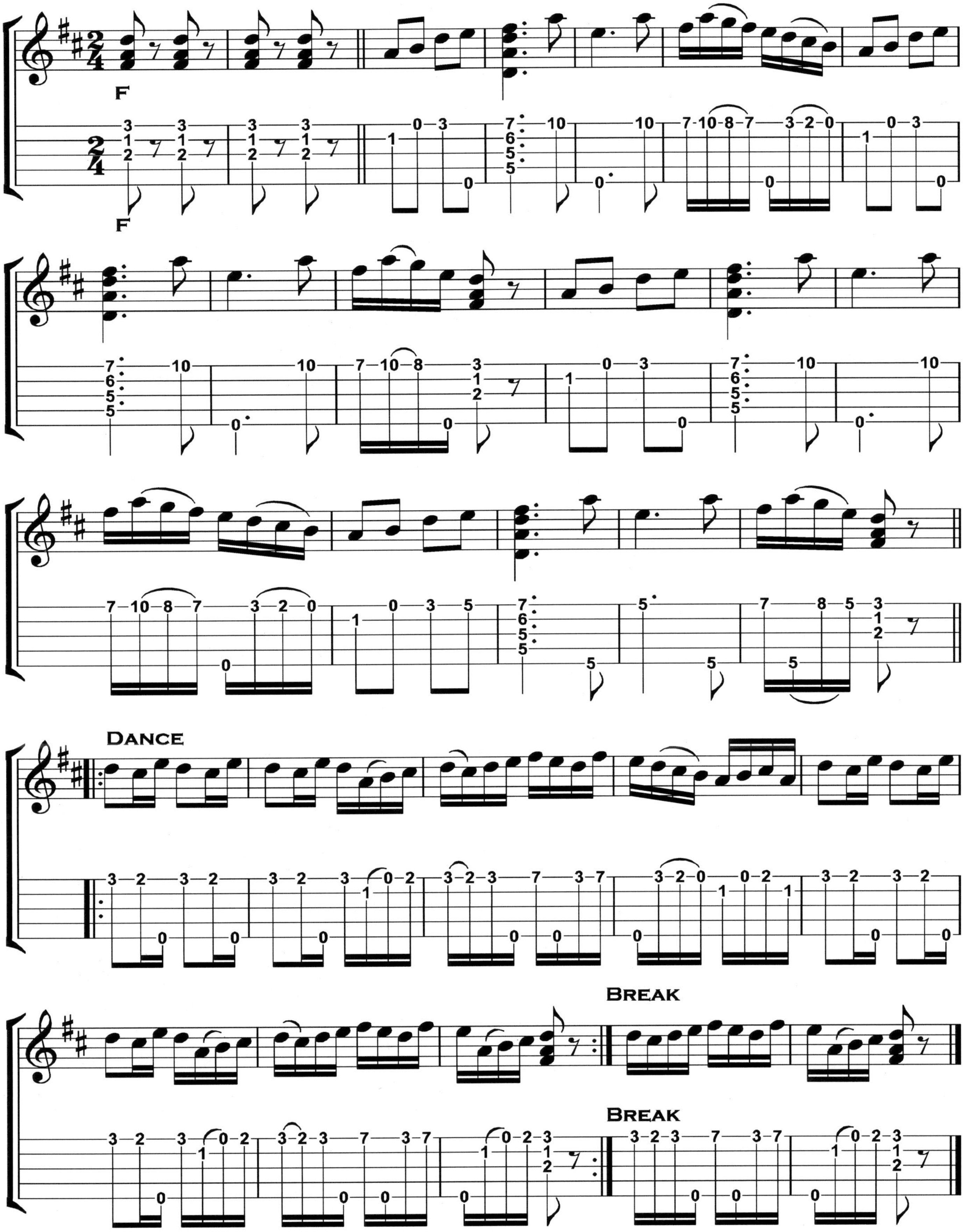

F

F

Dance

Break

Break

48
48. Medley Jig
Andante
Andante
1.
2. Fine

1.
2.
D.S. al Fine

49. Just the Thing Clog Dance

High 4th

50. Roll Down the Curtain Walk Around

F

Dance

Break

Other Mel Bay Recommended Banjo Books

Banjo Method: C Tuning (Bradbury)

Fun with the Banjo (M. Bay)

Fun with Strums/5-String Banjo (W. Bay)

Banjo and Chord Reference Wall Chart (J. Davis)

Scales and Arpeggios for Classical Banjo (Bullard)

Bach for the Banjo (Bullard)

Renaissance & Elizabethan Music for Banjo (Datesman)

Tarrant Bailey Jr. Banjo Solos: His Life and Works (Sands)

Early American Banjo (Buckley/Twiss)

Early American Classics for Banjo (MacKillop)

Early Irish-American Banjo (MacKillop)